Index It Right!

Advice from the Experts

Volume 1

Art
Biographies
Computer Manuals
Encyclopedias
Gardening/Horticulture
Philosophy
Theology
Web Sites

EDITED BY ENID L. ZAFRAN

AMERICAN
SOCIETY OF
INDEXERS

First Printing, 2005

Index It Right! Advice from the Experts, Volume 1

ISBN 1-57387-237-7

Published by
Information Today, Inc.
143 Old Marlton Pike
Medford, NJ 08055

in association with

The American Society of Indexers, Inc.
10200 West 44th Avenue
Suite 304
Wheat Ridge, CO 80033

Printed in the United States of America

President and CEO: Thomas H. Hogan, Sr.
Editor-in-Chief and Publisher: John B. Bryans
Managing Editor: Amy Reeve
VP Graphics and Production: M. Heide Dengler
Book Designer: Kara Mia Jalkowski
Copyeditor: Pat Hadley-Miller
Proofreader: Dorothy Pike
Indexer: Carrie Nearing

Contents

List of Figures

Introduction

Enid L. Zafran

The number of areas in which indexers work is as large and varied as the subject categories and formats of the books and information that fill our libraries and computers. Take, for example, the list of subject specialties from which members of the American Society of Indexers (ASI) can pick when registering their services with the Indexer Locator—more than 75 topics appear there. And then there are the types of material—the Locator enumerates 24 varieties. These lists are not close-ended; they continue to expand as new fields such as the Internet emerge, and with them the possibility for new formats like taxonomies and Web sites. Indexers find expanding opportunities for their skills as information becomes more complex and more essential.

I conceived of the idea for this series of *Index It Right* volumes as a vehicle for indexer-experts to discuss how they work in their fields of endeavor. Each article contains practical tips that will help those starting out in these specialties, and will continue to educate those already writing indexes in these areas. When you Index It Right, you know you have done the best job possible—you have joined the rank of experts!

For each subject in this book, I chose an expert who was willing to share his or her knowledge. I thank them all for their generosity in writing these articles. Although indexers find it a treat to create full sentences after years of writing short phrases, they rarely have the time in their work schedules to fulfill such obligations. However, the literature on indexing will only be worthwhile if developed by the actual practitioners of the art; theoreticians know little about the actual crafting of index structure. Likewise, subject experts (or authors) are not the most qualified people to write indexes. Authors typically do not have the skills to organize the material, the objectivity to treat the material fairly, or the viewpoint of the novice who is likely to use the index for information. The people to instruct others how to *Index It Right* are indexers.

The fields of this first volume are philosophy, theology, biography, horticulture, art, encyclopedias, computer manuals, and Web sites. The mix alone shows the richness and diversity of the indexing profession. Although some themes repeat from one article to the next (such as the proper form of name entries or making decisions due to space constraints), the approaches can vary. In art catalogs, names of artists and artworks drive the organization, while in encyclopedia indexing names need more selective handling due to numerous passing mentions and overlap. Although you may be drawn to the articles on the fields in which you work, I recommend that you take the time to look at the others. Maybe you have been reluctant to try indexing in one of these areas, and the article will give you needed confidence. I have worked in some of these fields and wished for just such accessible and sensible advice.

For instance, Carol Roberts, on indexing philosophy in Chapter 1, provides information that makes this task much less daunting. The abstraction of the subject matter can frighten those unsure about the field, whether they are creating useful entries or just wallowing in jargon. Carol has indexed many books in this field and urges the tentative indexer to include the odd-sounding entries for such phrases as "brain in a vat."

Kate Mertes has written about the related field of theology in Chapter 2. Kate has certainly become one of the best (if not "the best") indexers in the realm of theology. When I recently indexed an encyclopedia of Christian theology, I consulted Kate on several occasions to help me choose the best wording for subject headings. When you read her article, you will see why I valued her input.

Moving from the ethereal realm to that of physical objects, the contrast between philosophical/theological indexing and art indexing is striking. I have done quite a bit of art catalog indexing, so I found Susan DeRenne Coerr's description in Chapter 5 of the types of art books and the categories of information they contain to be most instructive. Susan's many examples of how to deal with untitled pieces, unnumbered illustration pages, and level of detail provide a how-to text for indexers in this field.

Art catalogs are notorious for devoting little space to the index, and it appears that gardening book indexers face a similar situation. Plant names use many variants, both in English and Latin. Just as famous paintings or artists become known by nicknames or shortened forms of their full names, so plants have other "aliases." In Chapter 6, Thérèse Shere, with the assistance of Lina Burton, has compiled guidance on what to do when the publisher will not allow space for all the variants to be included.

Although lack of space is not usually the challenge for the biography indexer, the organization of a person's life does not fall into the nice compartments that an indexer would like. The structure of the index will drive its usefulness in a biography. Martin White, in Chapter 3, analyzes the types of headings from indexes he has compiled, as well as from other books, such as the recent autobiography of Bill Clinton, which generated much controversy in the indexing community due to its inadequacies.

Moving from the narrow realm of biography and art books, Marion Lerner-Levine's article in Chapter 4 on encyclopedia indexing shows that the indexer of such works has to take a "big picture" approach. Encyclopedia indexing has special requirements (how to treat the subject of the article vs. how to treat the same figure in another article) for indexing treatment as well as for indexing format. Marion walks us through the process she followed for *Collier's Encyclopedia*, and we gain an appreciation for what goes into the updating and revision of such a large index.

In the more technical realm, articles come from Beth Palmer and Fred Brown in Chapters 7 and 8, respectively. Beth focuses on indexing computer manuals and gives a usability test to evaluate whether the index is doing its job. After all the discussions I have attended on how to judge the quality of an index, I found the simplicity of this procedure most refreshing. Its application can easily extend to other fields and provide a cost-effective method to validate your product.

Chapter 8 brings us to the electronic world of Web site indexing. Fred Brown looks at various portals and the linking methodologies they have created. Their schemes can be so simplistic that all they do is to take the user to another gateway page. They do not link to the actual information because that information undergoes constant change and the Web-site personnel do not want to incur the overhead to keep those links current. Clearly, this type of indexing is in a "larval" stage. Imagine if the book index only pointed to the table of contents and from there the user was left on her own! It is not likely that electronic researchers will put up with this half-baked approach for long. Fred's demonstration of what is currently available provides a baseline for future work in this area.

Each of these eight articles makes its own contribution to the literature of indexing. They demonstrate best practices, criticize shortcomings, and provide seasoned advice. By reading them and learning from them, you will be able to Index It Right!

Chapter 1

If a Tree Falls in the Forest: Indexing Philosophy Books

Carol Roberts © 2005

Broadly speaking, philosophy is the study of fundamental concepts and questions. Its scope is enormous: what we know and how we know it; existence of an external world (e.g., whether that falling tree makes a sound); the meaning of life; animal rights; beauty; existence of God; logic; euthanasia; and so on.

Books on philosophy fall into roughly two categories: popular philosophy (for a general audience) and scholarly philosophy (for philosophy professors and their graduate students). Pirsig's *Zen and the Art of Motorcycle Maintenance* is an example of the former, and Kant's *Critique of Pure Reason* is an example of the latter.

Philosophy writing, whether popular or scholarly, comes to us from three main traditions: Western analytic, Continental, and Eastern. Virtually all scholarly philosophy written in English-speaking countries is Western analytic. That's not to say that English-speaking philosophers don't discuss subjects like Buddhism or Hegelian ethics. But their approach follows the Western analytic style.

This essay will focus on indexing scholarly Western analytic philosophy for three reasons: scholarly philosophy is where the greatest difficulties lie; American, British, and Australian publishers would, for the most part, be offering you Western analytic philosophy; and, that's where my expertise applies. Popular philosophy should be manageable by most trained, intelligent indexers without any special background or preparation in philosophy. From here on, unless I indicate otherwise, assume the focus is on scholarly Western analytic philosophy.

WHO WRITES THIS STUFF?

Philosophy books have a reputation for being dense and full of jargon. That is, they are packed with concepts, which are expressed in a specialized language, as the following short passage shows:

> This division within Mill's theory between analysis and justifica-
> tion is important for a proper contrast between his view and ordinary
> rule-utilitarianism. The rule-utilitarian begins by formulating his basic
> principle as a moral principle, linking the moral appraisal of conduct
> indirectly to the promotion of happiness or welfare.[1]

I won't analyze this passage. The point of including it is that it illustrates typical scholarly philosophical writing. The sentences are, in and of themselves, perfectly readable albeit conceptually dense.

Why do philosophers write this way? Why don't they explain terms like "rule-utilitarianism"? Are they just elitist, trying to prevent the rest of us from understanding them? Or worse, is it meaningless gibberish? They do it because they are writing for their peers. Philosophy jargon, as in any specialized field, provides a kind of shorthand for concepts that professionals are already familiar with and don't need to define for each other every time. In popular philosophy, the jargon would still be there (although a bit less intensively), but the terms would be defined.

Aside from the difficulty of understanding the jargon, notice how densely packed the concepts are. That one paragraph discusses six different concepts (plus a name): analysis, justification, rule-utilitarianism, moral appraisal, happiness, and welfare. All of them (and the relationships among them) get indexed. Right away you can see how easy it is to accumulate upward of 10 indexable terms per page, something to keep in mind when setting a fee.

Philosophy can be woefully dry. Fair enough, but it can also be full of wit, as in these samples: "[L]ike many philosophers, I am of the school that what goes without saying often goes even better *with* saying" and "Indeed, [Kymlicka] thinks Rawls has not just left the door open to [culture as a good] but sat it down and served it tea."[2] The writing style and skill vary from one philosopher to the next.

But in general, it must be confessed that the language of professional philosophers is as verbose as it is sophisticated. If, on top of that (or because of that), it strikes you as pretentious or (worse) phony, then you might not be cut out for philosophy indexing. Not because you lack the skills or couldn't acquire them, but simply because you won't enjoy it.

SHOULD YOU OR SHOULDN'T YOU?

If you have some background in philosophy and enjoy reading it, then there's no reason not to index philosophy books. Even though some of the books may be esoteric, you'll be familiar enough with the analytic approach not to be alienated by the language.

What if you have no background in philosophy? There are several things you can do to prepare:

- Start with popular philosophy.

- Read some philosophy anthologies written for undergraduates, which you can pick up in college bookstores. This will familiarize you with the analytic approach, the different branches of philosophy, and the key figures in the history of philosophy. The history is very important, because so much of contemporary philosophical writing builds on the greats of the past, such as Plato, Aristotle, Locke, Hume, Descartes, and Aquinas. The best "Introduction to Philosophy" books are those written by philosophers for use in undergraduate courses. Steer clear of those written by nonphilosophers (check the author's credentials). I recommend these titles to get you started:

  - *Introduction to Philosophy: Classical and Contemporary Readings,* by John Perry and Michael Bratman (Oxford University Press, 3rd ed., 1998)

  - *Thinking It Through: An Introduction to Contemporary Philosophy,* by Kwame Anthony Appiah (Oxford University Press, 2003)

  - *What Does It All Mean? A Very Short Introduction to Philosophy,* by Thomas Nagel (Oxford University Press, 1987)

- Allow plenty of extra time for your first philosophy indexing projects.

NUTS AND BOLTS
The Argument Clinic

Man: Well, an argument's not the same as contradiction.

Mr. Vibrating: It can be.

Man: No it can't. An argument is a connected series of statements intended to establish a definite proposition.

Mr. Vibrating: No it isn't.

Man: Yes it is. It isn't just contradiction.

Mr. Vibrating: Look, if I argue with you, I must take up a contrary position.

Man: But it isn't just saying "No it isn't."

Mr. Vibrating: Yes it is.

Man: No it isn't, an argument is an intellectual process . . . contradiction is just the automatic gainsaying of anything the other person says.[3]

Think of a philosophy book as a 300-page argument. Broadly speaking, this argument will contain a thesis or theory about a subject, counterarguments (that is, reasons why the thesis might be wrong), what other philosophers have said about it, and (sometimes) why we should care about it.

To index a philosophy book, it's not necessary that you understand the argument in all its glorious details. However, it is important that you understand the general problem the author is addressing, which is usually spelled out in the introduction.

When Philosophers Duke It Out

An author may focus on a particular philosophical problem or subject or on particular philosophers who wrote about it. It's a judgment call whether the subject or the philosopher who wrote about it should be made into entries. Ask yourself where the focus of the passage is.

If the text says "Jeremy Bentham, whom Mill describes as," clearly the focus is on Bentham per se, not on a particular argument or subject he wrote about. In that case, you would double-post one under the other:

> Bentham, Jeremy
>> Mill on
> Mill, John Stuart
>> on Bentham

But if two philosophers are arguing about the same problem, keep it simple. Instead of this:

> justice
>> Nozick on
>> Rawls on
> Nozick, Robert
>> on Rawls's conception of justice
> Rawls, John
>> on Nozick's conception of justice

do this:

> justice
>> Nozick on
>> Rawls on
> Nozick, Robert
>> on justice
> Rawls, John
>> on justice

It's understood that for any given topic, such as justice, many philosophers have contributed to the pot and that each is responding to earlier authors. So it's usually not necessary in subentries to identify the target of a response. Whatever Rawls wrote about justice, he was interested in justice per se not just on Nozick's comments about it.

On the other hand, a good philosophical brawl concerns the people as well as the issues. If the passage deals with Gassendi's views on clear and distinct ideas, it is also about the famous dispute between Gassendi and Descartes. Depending on what other subs you have for Gassendi, you might need to index it both ways, simply because philosophers will associate Gassendi with Descartes just as much as with the content of the dispute:

> Gassendi, Pierre
> > on clear and distinct ideas
> > on Descartes

or

> Gassendi, Pierre
> > vs. Descartes, on clear and distinct ideas

It isn't necessary to capture Gassendi's precise views on clear and distinct ideas. Because philosophical writing is so meticulous and nuanced, it may be tempting to write long subentries in order to capture this nuanced language, but that doesn't help the reader locate information more precisely. The phrasing "Gassendi: on clear and distinct ideas as representations of objects outside the mind" doesn't get the reader to the right information in the text any better than "Gassendi: on clear and distinct ideas."

Following that reasoning, why not just "Gassendi: on ideas"? "Clear and distinct ideas" is a single concept. A good philosophy dictionary will be very valuable for learning how concepts are phrased and which ones form inseparable noun phrases.

Isms

Just about any term ending in "ism" is a philosophical concept and should be indexed: realism, idealism, existentialism, dialectical materialism, determinism, and so on. These are the low-hanging fruit of philosophy indexing, because they're easy to spot.

The text may talk about "ists" along with "isms." For consistency, it's usually best to choose one form throughout. I think of the ism as being the broader category than its adherents (the ists), so I prefer using the ism form.

Expert Tip

The types of subentries you might have under the isms could be a personal name, a definition, a comparison with another ism, or other related issues.

idealism
    Berkeley on
    definition of
    and God's omniscience
    vs. realism

It's important to index who is speaking about which isms. So in addition to creating main headings for isms, you'll need to include them as subentries:

Berkeley, George
    idealism of

or sometimes

Berkeley, George
    on idealism

Other Concepts

Other concepts present more of a challenge, simply because they don't include that helpful "ism" ending. Don't let these other concepts intimidate you. It's no different from picking out concepts in other scholarly fields; they just have strange names:

a priori truths [sort on the "a"]
categorical imperative
counterfactuals
existential import
is–ought gap
that than which nothing greater can be thought [index on "that," believe it
    or not]
evil demon

What if you know more or less what the author is talking about, but the concept isn't named? Or what if the author has used so many variants, you can't tell what the "official" concept term is? A good place to look for a term you can latch on to is in the endnotes. For example, the text talks about "positive state beneficence at the expense of autonomy." Although clearly the passage is about autonomy, it's also about something else, which the author has not named explicitly. So you check the endnote associated with the passage (philosophers use so many endnotes there's usually one you can check) and it says, "For more on paternalism, see . . . ." Voilà! The passage is about paternalism. That's not to say you would index the endnote (not if it was only a citation and didn't say anything substantive about paternalism), but nine times out of ten, you can rely on it to find that elusive concept term.

What Not to Index

Resist the temptation to create main headings for broad categories like these:

> arguments
> definitions
> examples
> fallacies

unless, of course, there is discussion of these subjects per se. For example, in a book about logic, there might well be some actual discussion of fallacies meriting indexing.

Philosophers vs. Philosophies

Be careful not to conflate philosophers with philosophies based on their theories. Philosophers expand on the work of their predecessors, and the scope of resulting theories can exceed the original theory. Or they may have gone in such a different direction that the original philosophers would be spinning in their graves. Keep these sorts of pairs separate, unless the author conflates them:

> Freud vs. Freudianism (or Freudian psychology or psychoanalysis)
> Descartes vs. Cartesianism
> Marx vs. Marxism
> Aristotle vs. Aristotelianism
> Plato vs. Platonism (or Neoplatonism or Platonic Forms)

"See also" references from philosophers to the isms based on their work can be very helpful, especially if they're separated in the index, for example,

> Descartes, René. *See also* Cartesianism

The Philosopher Formerly Known as Aristotle

Believe it or not, "the Philosopher" refers to Aristotle, just as "the Indexer" might be said to refer to Carol Roberts (I wish!). Contemporary philosophers always name Aristotle, but you may see this expression in quotations from medieval writers.

Distinctions Between Concepts

Distinctions between concepts are practically the hallmark of Western analytic philosophy. Watch for phrases like these: "the distinction between"; "versus"; "as opposed to." Paired concepts can be indexed in this format (double-posted):

> idealism: vs. realism
> realism: vs. idealism

If you're lucky, the author will make the distinction very apparent. This kind of wording is as good as it gets:

> The distinction about individualism in the sphere of rights is between what we can call *ethical* individualism on the one hand, and *substantive* individualism, on the other.[4]

which yields this entry:

> individualism: ethical vs. substantive

Schools of Thought and Groups of Philosophers

You may need to include cross-references to individual followers of a school of thought (if the text tells you who they are):

> Frankfurt School
> Vienna Circle. *See also* Gödel, Kurt

If the text talks about the school of thought but doesn't name any of its adherents, don't index them (except where they might be discussed elsewhere in the book). That would be overkill.

Fallacies

Fallacies also have names and merit their own entries:

> gambler's fallacy
> informal fallacy
> naturalistic fallacy

Some of them are given in the reverse order. It's a good idea to double-post these if there's space:

> fallacy of affirming the consequent
> affirming the consequent, fallacy of

You Bet Your Burridan's Ass

Philosophers use a lot of examples, analogies, and arguments, often giving them names. Go ahead and index the names, no matter how odd they sound.

> Burridan's ass
> brain in a vat
> Gettier problems
> Schrödinger's cat
> Zeno's paradoxes

These are classic examples of odd names that were unknown at the time they were introduced. In this passage, the author creates new philosophical terminology: "Because here a gaze can turn to stone, we can call this the Medusa Syndrome."[5] You might ask, "Why index Medusa Syndrome? The author just invented that term, so no one will look it up."

Expert Tip

Keep in mind that there are two audiences: those who haven't read the book and those who have. People who've already read the book may very well look up the invented terms they remember.

What if the author constructs a lengthy example and doesn't give it a name at all? How do you index that? The best way of handling this situation is to create a name and flag the entry so the author can either OK it or substitute another name. For example,

> zombie example {OK? or do you want to call it something else?}

The bulk of Judith Thomson's famous article on abortion is an analogy: You've been kidnapped and strapped to a sick violinist who needs to use your kidneys for nine months. As far as I know, Thomson didn't give the example a name, but other philosophers called it simply the "violinist example," and that's how it's known today. Choose a name that someone who has read the example might look it up under.

Arguments that do have formal names should be indexed by those names. Without a background in philosophy (and sometimes even with) you can't always tell if the argument's name is traditional or invented by the author on the spot. Go ahead and index them by name regardless. Here are a few traditional ones:

> argument from design
> argumentum ad hominem [itals. rarely used any more for these Latin names]
> free will problem
> mind/body problem *or* mind-body dualism [In some books, this will be
>   synonymous with "Cartesian dualism," but not always; be cautious]
> Ockham's razor
> reductio ad absurdum [sometimes just called a reductio]

Ecce Confusio

As if jargon weren't enough, philosophers like to pepper their writing with foreign phrases. The most common languages used are German, Greek, and Latin. The easiest case to deal with is the foreign phrase given with its translation, as in this excerpt on Kant: "On a 'pre-Copernican' view, objects are considered just by themselves, i.e., as 'things-in-themselves' (*Dinge an sich*)."[6] Because philosophers use both terms, these pairs are best handled by double-posting:

> *Dinge an sich* (things-in-themselves)
> things-in-themselves (*Dinge an sich*)

The usual rules regarding when to double-post and when to cross-reference apply here. That is, cross-reference when you have subentries or several locators. I would use the term that is not in parentheses as the preferred term. If the author uses the foreign term later in roman type, that means the italics were used only to introduce the term, so you would index it in roman.

Books on ancient Greek philosophy will, of course, contain many Greek words, which are often transliterated, as in this snippet on Aristotle: "The end of all action, the good for man, is happiness (*eudaimonia*)."[7]

> Aristotle: on happiness
> happiness: Aristotle on
> *eudaimonia. See* happiness

If the author has retained the Greek letters, the press will *probably* not expect you to index the Greek terms at all, and you can simply focus on the English concepts.

Quite a few Latin terms are used, often untranslated: "If, unlike BonJour, the coherence theorist extends his theory to encompass a priori knowledge, this argument will show that, on a coherentist approach, we have no a priori knowledge either."[8] The Latin phrase here includes the "a," which is not an article, so it's *not* ignored in sorting and would have to be sorted manually or force-sorted:

> a priori knowledge: coherentists on [here's a case in which it's best to use
> "ists" rather than "isms"]
> coherentists: on a priori knowledge

One of the most famous phrases in philosophy (in this case Latin) is "Cogito ergo sum," which means, "I think, therefore I am." In a scholarly book, it is often called simply "the cogito" (sometimes capped: "the Cogito"), and the author might not even bother translating it. It's important to trust philosophers to know their audience. If the author does not translate the phrase, that's because it's well understood by her or his peers, and your adding a translation would make the index appear fussy or, worse, dumbed down.

Not every foreign phrase represents an indexable concept. You wouldn't index, for example, "mutatis mutandis"; that would be like indexing "et cetera."

REFERENCE BOOKS AND WEB SITES

By now you should be thinking, "I'm going to need some kind of dictionary to understand all the foreign phrases and other jargon." Bingo! A good philosophy dictionary—whether sitting on your bookshelf or consulted online—will be extremely useful not only for sorting out terminology but for getting an overview of the philosophical problem your author is examining. A little bit of advance reading is time well spent if it gives you the gist of the problem as well as who the big names in your text are likely to be.

The following list includes both an affordable dictionary for at-home use, volumes you're more likely to consult in a library, and online resources. I would recommend that you sample these and determine which are readable for you.

> *The Cambridge Dictionary of Philosophy*, edited by Robert Audi
> (Cambridge University Press, 1995). I can't say enough about this
> dictionary. If you can buy only one philosophy reference book, this is
> the one. It's a whopping 882 pages long and is very readable. It contains an index of selected names and a useful appendix of special
> symbols and logical notation.

The Encyclopedia of Philosophy, edited by Paul Edwards (Macmillan, 1973), in 8 volumes. This is a very valuable set but, unless you were lucky enough to acquire it years ago through the Literary Guild, not very affordable. Many university libraries include it in their reference departments.

The Routledge Encyclopedia of Philosophy, edited by Edward Craig (Routledge, 1998), in 10 volumes (also on CD-ROM). I haven't seen it, but the reviews are very good, and Routledge's reputation is top-notch. Look for it in university libraries.

Stanford Encyclopedia of Philosophy is an online encyclopedia at http://plato.stanford.edu/contents.html. This useful site contains both a search engine and an index. Search results display summaries of the term's use, with links to articles.

The American Philosophical Association Web site contains a page of links to philosophy publishers. (http://www.apa.udel.edu/apa/asp/publishers.asp)

The Ism Book is an online dictionary that contains indexes by letter and also by area of philosophy. The entries give not only the definition of each ism but also its relationship to other isms. How valuable is that?! (http://www.saint-andre.com/ismbook/about-ism.html)

Philosophy Pages is a nice online collection of resources, including a dictionary, study guide, and timeline. The study guide in particular would prove very useful for indexers without a background in philosophy. (http://www.philosophypages.com)

ENDNOTES

1. David Lyons, *Rights, Welfare, and Mill's Moral Theory* (Oxford University Press, 1994), p. 78.
2. Kwame Anthony Appiah, *The Ethics of Identity* (Princeton: Princeton University Press, 2005), pp. xvi and 121, respectively.
3. "The Argument Clinic," Monty Python's Flying Circus (BBC Television, 1971).
4. Appiah, p. 72.
5. Appiah, p. 110.
6. *The Cambridge Dictionary of Philosophy,* edited by Robert Audi (Cambridge University Press, 1995), p. 400.
7. *The Cambridge Dictionary of Philosophy,* p. 44.
8. Robert J. Fogelin, *Pyrrhonian Reflections on Knowledge and Justification* (Oxford University Press, 1994), p. 168n.7

Chapter 2

The Queen of Sciences: Indexing Theology and Disciplines Related to Religion

Kate Mertes © 2005

Thomas Aquinas called theology the "queen of sciences," using science in its medieval sense of a pursuit of knowledge or a knowledge base. In his day most people assumed that all intellectual action came down to questions about God, and in practice that was pretty much the case. Climb into your time machine and take a ramble through the Bodleian Library in Oxford any time before about 1550, unchain and open any of the small collection of books it contained, and you'd almost certainly be reading about a religious topic.

After that, of course, things began to change. Now most people regard theology as a rather obscure topic. Indeed, Stephen Hawking, in *A Brief History of Time* (New York: Bantam, 1998), felt emboldened enough to state that physics has usurped theology's crown, taking over as the discipline that answers the ultimate questions about who we are and why we are here. Whether or not you agree with him that we have a new queen of sciences, there's no doubt that many people are uninterested in, and even uncomfortable with, the kinds of religious questions that once excited the world. Even in Middle Eastern and Asian cultures, which tend to be more directly oriented to spiritual issues than are our secular Western societies, it's hard to imagine a city in which the chief talk in the taverns and on the street corners is of the edicts of the Council of Chalcedon and the divine nature of Christ, as was the case in Byzantine Constantinople.

Nevertheless, society continues to crave spiritual writings, even if it's the platitudes of *Chicken Soup for the Teenage Soul* or the ersatz mysticism of *The Da Vinci Code*. If they were in the running, the Bible and the Quran would always be on the *New York Times* bestseller list. Jews, Christians, and Muslims are not known as "people of the book" for nothing. Theology and spirituality remain living academic disciplines, with new schools of thought (feminist philosophy of religion, liberation theology) in constant development. Non-Western theological works now appeal to worldwide audiences. Religious topics already make up a hefty portion of the bookselling market and are the fastest growing segment of the publishing industry (*Publisher's Weekly,* 8/2/2004).

The vast majority of these works need indexes, and indexers to write them. Yet because of perceptions of difficulty, yawn-inducing tendencies, and simple disinterest in religious subject matter, many indexers are reluctant to tackle theological works. I've often had lucrative and interesting projects referred to me by indexers who are just afraid to handle writings about God. This article is an attempt to help indexers take a second look at theology and other religious disciplines. The field has economic potential, as well as the intellectual stimulation indexers crave.

WHAT IS THEOLOGY?

First, however, it might be useful to define terms. What is theology? There's both a specific and a loose use of this word. Etymologically, "theology" is derived from the Greek *theos logos,* or study of God. Most frequently the term is used to describe the study of religious practice, belief, and experience as an academic discipline, particularly when approached in a systematic way. (Thus, "theology" can also be used to indicate a specific belief system.) Academic theology is particularly associated with analyses of the nature of God and God's relationship to the world. Not surprisingly, theology is closely associated with theistic conceptions of religious belief, in which God is framed as having some sort of personal identity.

"Theology" can also be defined in a much, much looser sense, to cover any religious topic at any level, theistic or nontheistic. Used in this way, it's sometimes described as "talk about God," encompassing everything from the writings of Deepak Chopra to the works of Theodore of Mopsuestia. From this perspective it would not be unusual to refer to Advaita Vedanta as "Sanskrit theology," even though it has no concept of God in a personal sense. (See Paul J. Griffiths, "Nontheistic Conceptions of the Divine," *Oxford Handbook of Philosophy of Religion,* ed. William J. Wainwright, NY: OUP, 2005, pp. 59-79.) In this article, when I use the term "theology," I will generally be using it in this looser sense. If I use it in a more specific sense, I will generally refer to it as "academic theology."

One problem that some people have with theology as a discipline is that it usually, although not always, takes place within a framework of belief. Indeed, an old Catholic definition of theology is "faith seeking understanding." This is not unique to theology; many scholars in other disciplines base their work on a foundation of accepted knowledge, whether it's Darwinian evolutionary theory or deconstructionism. But much, though not all, "talk about God" grows out of a corpus of revelatory wisdom subject to limited questioning. The degree of dependence on revelation varies enormously, but it remains a factor central to the understanding of any theological text.

CULTURAL MILIEU AND PERSONAL BELIEF

Indexers are well aware of the challenges inherent in indexing both familiar and unfamiliar disciplines. When we are closely attuned to subject matter, we may miss or ignore common sense or everyday language in favor of jargon that we don't even recognize as such. I'm using jargon here in its nonpejorative sense, to mean the specialized vocabulary common to a specific discipline. Jargon makes talking about a subject easier. My 75-year-old mother recently got her first computer, and explaining even simple operations was at first problematic; she didn't know what a diskette is, for instance. I had to think through the specialized language about computers I now take for granted in order to get ideas across to her. We can communicate about computers much more easily now that she has begun to pick up the language.

The other danger of growing comfortable with a particular topic is that it becomes fatally easy to structure the index using the classical ideologies of that discipline. As someone both brought up Roman Catholic and trained as a medievalist and a Roman Catholic theologian, I inevitably think about sacraments, for instance, in a certain way and even in a certain order. But that may not correspond at all to the way the reader thinks about them, and the way I structure the index may not, therefore, be helpful. Alternatively, the author might be proposing a radical approach to the topic, on which I might be tempted to impose a structure that is traditional to the discipline, but that just doesn't work for this particular study of it.

Indexers seldom are a perfect intellectual match for the books they are hired to do, so it's perhaps more common for us to find ourselves working on an alien topic or on an aspect or perspective of a discipline with which we are not familiar. This lack of sophistication may serve a purpose if the product in question is aimed at a beginning audience, but becomes more of a problem when it is composed at an advanced level. We all know the pitfalls here, and every indexer has worked out ways of dealing with them. We don't know the jargon; sometimes we don't even recognize that the jargon *is* jargon (I once knew an indexer who got halfway through a book on pension benefit plans before discovering that "defined benefit plans" meant a specific type of retirement arrangement); the book's argumentative structure may appear wholly foreign; and we may have to struggle to avoid applying a more familiar intellectual approach to a strange topic.

These problems occur in every field within which indexers work, but they are especially at issue in theology. Assumptions about religious belief, practice, and spirituality form part of the deep structure of all cultures, which makes it hard to be aware of them in the conscious manner required of the diligent indexer. This may be especially true of our secular society, where God and talk about God doesn't live on the surface of the world. Certainly I have found it easier to explain the notion of theism to people from Asian religious traditions than to get across nontheistic concepts of God to Westerners.

Moreover, because theology is so often practiced from a standpoint of belief, it tends to carry a lot of baggage with it, even in supposedly uncomplicated texts. Like a poor-performing airline carrier, indexers may find themselves losing track of all those suitcases full of background information rolling down the intellectual conveyor belt, and important topics may find themselves wandering disconsolately around the airport terminal of the index, permanently separated from their related concepts. For instance, in a devotional book about the rosary, I found that the indexer had made an entry for the glorious mysteries, but none for the joyful or sorrowful mysteries. There were, however, entries for the scourging of Christ, and for the crucifixion, which are part of the sorrowful mysteries, and entries for the Assumption were not doubled-posted or cross-referenced under the glorious mysteries. If you have no idea what I am talking about, well—I suspect you have something in common with the indexer who worked on this book. It is intended to be a simple piece of writing for a general audience, but to someone outside its cultural milieu it must seem like indexing Chinese.

The prospective indexer of religious products may face any one of five situations in which the cultural milieu or personal beliefs of the book and the indexer raise difficulties in proceeding with the production of the index.

"I was brought up without any religious tradition whatsoever. How do I index theology?" I majored in medieval studies in college. One of my fellow students in this small cross-disciplinary program was the child of psychologists determined to raise their children free of the neuroses induced by religion. I was never certain of how they felt about their eldest child's four-year commitment to studying a world intimately related to belief processes. But I do know that my friend's biggest difficulty in pursuing her studies was her lack of familiarity with the kinds of assumptions and motivations of a world imbued with religious enculturation. Imagine trying to comprehend something like chantry endowments without any experience or sense of how the church can act upon human existence. This is not a matter of belief per se, but of cultural instantiation. I have been confidentially informed by Chinese colleagues that their students in China who study English literature spend their first semesters on the Bible; it's the only way they can get their minds around Milton's *Paradise Lost.* It's not simply a matter of having to master a foreign belief system, but of people raised in a secularized communist system handling the idea of any belief system. These same colleagues find that students with any sort of religious background tend to catch on more quickly to the underlying themes of classical Western literature.

Westerners without religious enculturation usually do not have the same problems reading *Paradise Lost,* of course. Its themes resonate throughout even our secular cultural life. However, tackling an index to a nonfiction text dealing with theology without any religious background may make one feel like the hapless Chinese students reading Milton: adrift without a paddle. However, indexers do have the materials to make a paddle out of their own cultural and social backgrounds. Theological issues are informed by the world in which they develop, the same world we live in, and recognizing that can help you understand more fully what the theologian is trying to do. The Dominican theologian Brian Davies once told me that the point of philosophy is a simple human goal: "How should we live?" How do we make moral decisions? How do we choose which path to take? At its heart theology is asking the kinds of questions that we all ask about how to best live a decent life, in a systematic way and from a perspective of faith.

"I was raised in Reform Judaism and I'm trying to index a book on Orthodox Jewish thought"—interdenominational indexing. Indexing a book on a topic within your own religious tradition but outside your specific denomination creates its own problems. On the one hand, you assume a certain level of familiarity with the basic dogmatics and principles of faith and practice. On the other hand, it's a bit like that old saw about England and the United States being two countries separated by a common language. Denominations may have different meanings for the same term, or know a similar concept under a different term altogether, or have quite divergent systems for organizing thought or classifying spiritual activity. Many of these potential pitfalls can be checked with a simple awareness of potential conflict. It's also worthwhile to have access to resources—dictionaries, encyclopedias, Web sites—that specifically deal with the theology of the denomination you're working on. You'll get a very different discussion of predestination, for instance, depending on whether you look it up in a Protestant vs. a Catholic source.

"I'm a Wesleyan Methodist and I'm working on a Muslim text"—inter-Abrahamic indexing. The so-called Abrahamic faiths—Jewish, Christian, Muslim—are very different, but they share a surprising number of assumptions about the nature of God. For instance, all three are theistic religions—God has a certain personal, present, humanized character, humans are viewed as created in God's image, and God works directly in our world. While Jews and Christians are pretty well aware of the inter-relationships between their religious doctrines, people are often surprised at how much theory and even story that Islam shares with Judaism and Christianity. Nevertheless, the wise indexer approaches a sister faith with caution. Jews and Muslims don't always understand the full theological ramifications of the Christian doctrine of the trinity, for instance, assuming that Christians are polytheists rather than monotheists. Christians often miss the relationship between praxis and theology as it functions in Judaism.

"I'm a Muslim trying to index a book on Buddhism"—indexing across belief systems. If the Abrahamic faiths must exercise caution in indexing across belief systems, East-West cross-indexing can be even more confusing. The most basic assumptions of Western religious systems can be quite foreign to Eastern faiths such as Buddhism, Hinduism, and Confucianism. Indeed, the very concept of theology as the study of the nature of God is somewhat alien in Eastern faiths, in which God is not necessarily a personalized being. Westerners also tend to assume that a religion like Hinduism, with its many manifestations of divinity, is a form of polytheism, whereas Hinduism holds that God is one (insofar as Hinduism conceives of God as a being of any sort).

Eastern religions have since the 1960s enjoyed a certain popularity in Western culture, and in some cases books apparently dealing with, say, Buddhist belief are in fact Westernized interpretations. Indexers need to understand the purpose and background of the author in order to approach the book from the proper perspective.

"I'm working on a topic within my own religious tradition, but it seems totally alien!" Despite claims of eternal verity and timelessness made by many if not most organized religions, belief and practice in fact vary infinitely and change constantly. Thus indexers may be surprised by texts that supposedly lie within a familiar tradition, but upon closer examination contain all sorts of new and strange elements. Some of these elements result from entirely new strains of thought within theology, while others are the fruit of interdisciplinary academe. Recent examples include:

- A spiritual guide to the stations of the cross that includes Buddhist meditative techniques

- An introduction to Kabbalah referencing modern psychosocial theory

- A history of Islam utilizing concepts drawn from current ideas about the experience of ethnicity

- A book about Hindu deities comparing them to Christian cults of saints

Indeed, whole shelves' worth of theological schools arise, evolve, and fade every decade. Indexers who want to work on theology regularly do well to keep up with the latest trends and influences, in order not to be thrown by the use of the latest buzzwords and pet theories in even the most traditional texts. Theological journals offer a good source of new ideas, but just reading the newspapers in the right frame of mind will keep the alert indexer attuned to evolving trends (such as the current celebrity mania for Kabbalah) that may turn up in theological projects.

Academic theology remains divisible into two major schools: analytic (or Anglo-American) theology, and Continental theology (a division paralleling analytic and Continental philosophy; see Carol Roberts' article, Chapter 1 in this volume). Analytic philosophy emphasizes logical analysis of concepts and ideas, and is the dominant strain of theological thought in the United States and the United Kingdom. Continental philosophy presents more of a grab bag than a united school of thought, signifying the methods and styles of a whole range of theologies practiced in Continental Europe, including phenomenology, existentialism, and deconstructionism. Continental philosophy could perhaps be said to study logical processes as much as it uses them. Awareness of these two major theological strains can help indexers get a better grip on new types of religious thought; it helps, for instance, to know that feminist theology charges analytic theory with fundamental criticisms and borrows heavily from Continental philosophy.

While Eastern philosophies and religions have exercised a tremendous pull on Western thought in the last 40 years, it is only recently that any sort of sophisticated approach to non-Western belief systems has evolved in Western literature (and African- and Native American religious beliefs remain obscure in most academic theological surveys). Nevertheless, indexers need to be aware of their potential influence on texts, either from a pop culture standpoint or from an academic approach. Most modern encyclopedias of theology now address Eastern religious thought. Even though these texts often try to frame Eastern philosophies in European knowledge systems, they can provide a useful guide to how Western thinkers (the authors of most of the texts indexers will be working on) use non-Western beliefs and practices.

LANGUAGE AND RELIGION

Do you like languages? Are you interested in things like etymology and the origins of language? Then you might do well at indexing theology. Theology is heavily involved with language. Both analytical and Continental philosophies delve into language theory and the study of religious language. Analytical philosophy was rejuvenated in the early 20th century by writers intent on teasing out the meaning and function of talk about God. Wittgenstein, one of the giants of Continental philosophy, closely related the language function to the human need for relationships, with each other and with God; his deconstruction of St. Augustine's description of learning to talk as a child has exercised enormous influence over both Anglo-American and European theologians. Advaita Vedanta, a school of Sanskrit religious thought, treats the actual vocalized syllables of the Veda texts as sacred objects.

Besides language theory, the indexer of theological works will need certain language skills. No, you don't actually have to be fluent in Hittite or Chaldean, or even Greek or Latin, to index most theological texts (although it might help in some cases). For one thing, there are just too many languages; detailed Biblical commentaries might reference texts in 17 or more languages and dialects. Publishers have decided that most modern readers don't want to struggle with vast chunks of untranslated dead languages, and they're probably right, so they insist that even authors who write academic tomes for specialists translate quoted passages and transliterate texts in, say, Arabic or Greek into the Latin alphabet. However, indexers do have to be comfortable with handling unfamiliar speech: recognizing significant terms, identifying and joining together different grammatical forms of the same word, and reproducing them accurately in the index. Indexers who wish to work on high-end academic projects, especially commentaries on religious works and historical texts, will find this much easier if they have at least some knowledge of Hebrew, Greek, and Latin. I have produced indexes for both Buddhist Chinese and Hindu theological works, and did not experience any hindrance from my total lack of knowledge of Chinese and my minimal familiarity with Sanskrit and Urdu; these works were created for a Western audience whose own linguistic skills were assumed to be minimal. I do, however, have a certain facility for recognizing how languages are put together, developed from exposure to a wide range of languages and from studying and indexing linguistics texts, an undoubtedly useful background for any indexer.

Even if terms are translated and transliterated, however, the indexer may have to deal with diacriticals (an accent mark associated with an orthographic figure to indicate a phonetic value, for instance, the ç in François or the é in fiancé). You can add certain diacriticals using the insert symbol function in most word processing and indexing software, but this can be clumsy and time-consuming if there are a lot of them, and I've never yet met a software package that covers all the diacriticals required in a complex theological text. Indexers may need to work out a diacriticals "cheat sheet," with unique codes for each accent and letter, which the project's production editor can then convert. It's good to warn the editor or author about this at the start of the project. Sometimes the editor will have already worked out such a set of codes; if not, the indexer can easily create one. Just remember that the code has to be a unique set of characters so you can do a global conversion without risk of false positives. If I have a lot of diacriticals I like to be systematic about it. I'll do all vowels with long accent lines over them as the appropriate vowel between pipes; for instance ā would be represented as |a|, ē as |e|. You would turn in the diacritical code list along with the final index.

Expert Tip

Indexers may need to work out a diacriticals "cheat sheet," with unique codes for each accent and letter, which the project's production editor can then convert.

BIAS, POLEMIC, AND APOLOGETICS

I mentioned earlier that the wise indexer keeps in mind that most theology is written from a perspective of faith. The author often is working not just with but also from within a belief system. Theologians are not divorced from the concept of intellectual balance in their work, but they do start out inside a certain framework, which inevitably colors their conclusions. In this way theology shares a certain commonality with political science and economics, fields in which academic writers often start from a specific point of view and with certain assumed values. Two recognized types of theological writing, polemic and apologetics, concern defending or attacking a particular set of beliefs. Apologetics is a systematic argument defending a specific doctrine (especially associated with early Christian writing); polemic is a systematic attack on a specific doctrine (such as Rabbi Abraham ibn Ezra's refutation of Christian Biblical exegesis, or Walter of St. Victor's *Contra quatuor labyrinthos Franciae*). This means that the theological indexer may have to deal with the problem of bias, sometimes crude, sometimes quite sophisticated.

In such situations it behooves indexers to remember their job—helping readers find information in the text. If the information is one-sided or poorly presented or even just offensive, well, that fortunately is not our problem. This may mean using more generally accepted terms that readers will more likely use rather than the text's specific terminology (albeit with appropriate cross-references). And tempting as it may be to imitate the indexer of a famous obstetrics/gynecology text who included the entry, "birds, for the, 1–495," when indexing some of the more virulent papal encyclicals, you should resist. You are not paid to give your own opinion when indexing. Sensitive souls can always opt to refuse a project due to its subject matter (not that you need to tell the editor or author that).

It is with good reason that English gentlemen were admonished not to bring up the topics of sex, politics, or religion at the dinner table; they tend to get everyone's ire up, and indexers are no exception. Indexers may find their own prejudices the hardest to deal with, rather than their authors', when indexing theology. Being the queen of sciences, theology deals with a wide range of potentially inflammatory subjects. Be it birth control, abortion, homosexuality, feminism, charity, or child abuse, theological texts stand a good chance of pushing all your buttons. But swallowing hard and representing the text fairly is one thing; bias can be a far more subtle issue than that. For instance, as a Catholic, I was raised with an idea of sainthood that is quite oppositional to Protestant ideas of the saints. When I index a non-Catholic text, I have to remain aware of the assumptions I bring to the table, and not use them to force ideas in the text into "Kate"-shaped boxes.

TYPES OF RELIGIOUS TEXT

The queen of sciences is a wide-ranging discipline, and the potential indexer of theological works will encounter many different sorts of texts to work on, of varying degrees of difficulty and aimed at all sorts of readerships. The simpler works are not necessarily the easiest to work on as far as indexing goes. Academic theology can be mind-bending to read, but well-organized enough that its indexing is not a struggle. Spiritual works, however, although aimed at a far more general audience, are often loosely organized and highly allusive as to subject matter. These works pose problems even to those familiar with such works and comfortable with their language and themes. Dictionaries and encyclopedias, although their length and range of subject matter make them formidable, probably constitute the easiest types of theological project for a "newbie" to handle. It's clear what the topic of each article is, terms are identified and defined, and the entire product aims to help people unfamiliar with the field. Those new to indexing, unless already comfortable with religious thought, should probably stay away from theology. Combining an untried skill with an unfamiliar subject area sounds like a bad idea because it is. For intrepid souls who want to give it a try, I provide the following summaries of some of the main types of theological texts.

Academic Theology

This is probably what most people think of when they imagine a theological work: a scholarly monograph systematically dealing with a religious concept, particularly one dealing with the nature of God. William Hasker's *God, Time, and Knowledge* (Ithaca, NY: Cornell University Press, 1989) is a classic example. It focuses on the traditional attributes of God shared by all of the Abrahamic faiths—omniscience, omnipotence, and divine goodness—and the logical problems these pose (such as, how does an all-powerful, all-seeing, and unlimitedly good God allow evil to exist in the world?). Indexers who specialize in scholarly texts, particularly those who happily index philosophy, should enjoy indexing academic theology.

Philosophy of Religion

Most academic theology could also be classified as philosophy of religion—philosophical works aimed at God and at religious belief. For earlier writers such as Aristotle, Thomas Aquinas, and John Locke, philosophy was pretty much inseparable from talk about God. Modern philosophical writers interested in religion tend to write more exclusively, and philosophy of religion tends to be a separate specialty (although relatively modern philosophers, such as Wittgenstein and Nietzsche, wrote extensively about religious belief in their more general philosophical works). The classic topic for religious philosophers is the existence of God, from Anselm of Canterbury to Immanuel Kant, but all sorts of theological topics appeal to philosophers. While an academic theologian might approach a topic such as miracles from a historical framework, or in terms of how belief in miracles interacts with a particular doctrine, a philosopher of religion would tend to be more interested in, say, questions of logical probability. The journal *Faith and Philosophy* and the *Oxford Handbook of Philosophy of Religion* (ed. William J. Wainwright, NY: OUP, 2005) provide useful guidance in this field.

The Bible

The Bible provides a branch of publishing all in itself. (Much of what I say about the Bible should apply to Quranic studies and to works on the canonical materials of other belief systems such as the Veda, albeit on a less extensive scale, but my own experience is mostly with Jewish and Christian Biblical theology, so I will restrict myself to discussing what I know best.) Most Bibles include a rudimentary index, but most of them don't begin to provide real access to the Biblical texts—see for instance the 15-page index in the standard edition of the *Jerusalem Bible* (first published in 1966), to a text that is 451 pages long. Technically it should be possible to produce a detailed, pinpoint Biblical index, using the standard chapters and verses as locators, which could be applied to any edition. However, the Bible (1) is very long; (2) its text is dense with information; (3) the text varies more than you might think between versions, and over time; and, perhaps most significantly; (4) the topics "read into" the Biblical text, which need to be indexed as much as the text itself, vary between religious traditions and over time, and are in any case implicit rather than explicit. Take, for instance, the Book of Daniel. Different parts of it are canonical (accepted as the inspired word of God) for different religions and denominations. The various translations (and I'm only dealing with English versions here) break the text up a little differently into the chapters and verses we tend to think of as fixed. And although, for a Christian, no index entry on foretellings of Christ would be complete without multiple references to Daniel, this book of the Bible has a whole different significance for Jews and Muslims.

Annotated Bibles—with scholarly notes providing information, historical context, definitions, and comments on the significance and interpretation of various passages—encompass a whole other level of information that requires indexing. I recently indexed a relatively straightforward annotated Bible aimed at Jews who were just beginning the process of Biblical study (*Jewish Study Bible,* Jewish Publication Society Tanakh Translation, ed. Adele Berlin, Marc Zvi Brettler, and Michael Fishbane, OUP, 2003). Only the commentary material was indexed, but I still had a hard time keeping the index under the required 50 pages. Nevertheless, it was an exhilarating experience. I've talked with William Meisheid, indexer and online help guru, about producing a universal Bible index, something we're both interested in pursuing.

Biblical commentaries present detailed studies of a Biblical text, usually single books and in some cases only parts of a book, or perhaps even a few crucial verses. Commentaries present many challenges for the indexer. They assume knowledge of many abstruse theological concepts, reference sources, and influences in multiple languages, and require tables of such things as Biblical quotations, ancient sources, and modern scholarly authors as well as a subject index. The contents of the commentary proper are often densely written and heavily footnoted. A good example, Jacob Milgrom's *Leviticus 23-27* (NY: Doubleday, 2000, part of the Anchor Bible Press series), consists of verse-by-verse commentary, plus essays on specific topics such as Leviticus' documentation of the transformation of the Israelite sacrificial system, the development of purification ritual, the concept of holiness in ancient Israel, and the idea of the "resident alien" as laid out in Levitical law. Commentaries can be exhausting to index, but provide a real sense of accomplishment on completion. Some commentaries are in fact commentaries upon commentaries, such as J. W. Bowker's *The Targums and Rabbinic Literature* (CUP, 1969).

Targums, Aramaic translations or paraphrases of and commentaries on texts from the Hebrew Bible, were derived from oral readings that were part of early synagogue practice, and preserved in written form. Both Jewish and Christian scholars rely on targum literature.

Spiritual Works

Although spiritual writings prove perhaps the most accessible type of religious text for many readers, in my opinion they are among the toughest works to index. Spiritual writing might be defined as any work that treats the individual's response to the call of faith. Such texts range from essentially practical guides to religious practice, such as a book of meditations on the Sacred Heart of Jesus, through popular inspirational works like Thomas Merton's *The Seven Storey Mountain* (NY: Harcourt, 1998), about a young man's entry into a Trappist Monastery, to intellectually challenging works including Elaine Pagel's *Beyond Belief* (NY: Random House, 2003), chronicling the international scholar's work on the Gospel of Thomas as it interplays with the ordeal of her infant son's critical illness. By their very nature, spiritual works seldom follow a straightforward, logical argument, and they are highly allusive, playing (often indirectly) on multiple cultural and religious leitmotifs—a bit like rap music, you find yourself chasing the samplings and sometimes missing the central themes.

Ritual Works

Missals, prayer books, psalmodies—almost all religions have ritual practices, many of which require written guidebooks to help worshippers through the readings, public prayers, and activities, and quite a few of these guidebooks need indexes. Ritual guides are fun and often quite easy to index—*if* you understand the religious practices they are meant to serve. If possible, attend the appropriate service with a veteran member of the congregation to grasp the function of a ritual work.

History and Archaeology

One of my favorite books of all time is Bernhard W. Anderson's *The Living World of the Old Testament* (Harlow, England: Pearson Education, 2000). First published in 1958, this book has gone through many printings and at least four editions. Anderson relates the Biblical text to the geography, history, and archaeology of the Middle East, using the latest research and scholarship. If you are a history or archaeology buff, you will enjoy this expansive wing of theological indexing. Some of the published material has a highly polemical flavor, especially the work of some Biblical scholars supported by religious groups bound and determined to use archaeology to prove theological points; but most works are essentially secular scholarly studies. Some travel literature is related to this category, such as Jerome Murphy-O'Connor's *The Holy Land* (OUP, 1998), another classic work now in its fourth edition (originally published in 1980). Although many of these texts are not theologically oriented, they nevertheless do require some knowledge of theological concepts. Shimon Gibson's *The Cave of John the Baptist* (NY: Doubleday, 2004), a study of the excavation of a cave used for ritual bathing as far back as the Iron Age and possibly associated with the baptismal practices of John the Baptist, necessarily discusses early Israelite purification rituals; first century *miqwot;* and Jewish, pagan, and early Christian notions of baptism. Other historical works are much more bound up with theological concepts: John P. Meier's *A Marginal Jew: Rethinking the Historical Jesus* (3 vols., NY: Anchor Bible, 1991-2001) attempts to place Jesus in his proper first century context with an extensive study of the religious and political world in which early Christianity incubated.

Premodern Works

Most religions rely heavily on tradition and the historical past, so premodern texts play a huge role in theological scholarship. Aside from canonical texts such as the Bible, the Quran, and the Veda, works such as the writings of Rabbi Moses Maimonides (a 12th-century Jewish commentator) and Thomas Aquinas (whose masterwork, the *Summa Theologia,* was written in the 13th century) still provided the framework for much modern theological writing. Such texts are objects of religious scholarship themselves and regularly produced in revised editions and new translations, both with and without additional commentary. The indexer has to work through multiple prisms, faithfully representing the concepts of the original authors and the culture and assumptions of the world in which they lived, the ideas of the modern editor, and the concerns of the current readership. I am currently working on a modern edition of Hugo Grotius' *De Iure Belli ac Pacis (The Laws of War and Peace)* (Liberty Fund, 2005), originally written in Latin in the 17th century (not strictly a theological text, but like many early modern works alight with talk about God). In the 18th-century English translation, by John Morrice, itself based on an earlier French translation by Jean Barbeyrac, I have to somehow render in the index the different uses of the term "liberty": Grotius' original conception of *libertas,* closer to our idea of free will; Barbeyrac's and Morrice's notes on *liberté* and "liberty," still not quite paralleling ours; the modern editor's comments on the developing concept of freedom, sometimes but not always related to the use of "liberty"; and finally, the modern readers' expectations. In addition, the particular mission of the text's publisher is to "foster thought and encourage discourse on enduring issues pertaining to liberty," which includes "the study of the ideal of a society of free and responsible individuals." Readers of Liberty Fund books tend to be especially interested in concepts of liberty and freedom and will look for them in the index. That's a great deal to hang on three little syllables. But that's the challenge and the job of working with historical materials.

Language Texts

Earlier I discussed the indexer's need for certain linguistic skills when working on any theological text. Some religious writings are in fact language texts. Serious Jewish and Christian scholars study Greek, Hebrew, Latin, and Aramaic, plus many more obscure languages such as Hittite, Chaldean, and Syriac. Muslim scholars and devotees read the Quran in Arabic; Western converts to Buddhism often desire to master a number of the languages of that religion's important texts. Language text-books are often written precisely for theological students and stress the vocabulary they require; instead of "la plume de ma tante," it's "l'argument d'ontologique de mon oncle" in these books! Depending on the level of expertise the book assumes on the part of the reader, the indexer may need anything from minimal to extensive knowledge of the language in question.

Still other texts could be classified as linguistic studies based largely or entirely on religious works. Many studies of the linguistic roots and lingering remnants of Aramaic are based on surviving Biblical fragments, for instance. Finally, philosophical studies of religious language—"the use of language in connection with the practice of religion," that is, to quote William P. Alston ("Religious Language" in *Oxford Handbook of Philosophy of Religion,* ed. William J. Wainwright, NY: OUP, 2005, p. 220), both talk *about* God and talk *to* God—form a whole subsection on the library shelves of divinity schools. These works may concern themselves with logical analysis of religious statements, or predicates; or they may stress the understanding and expression of religious concepts. Such texts require indexers to be comfortable with linguistic theory, philosophical musings, and theological topics.

Expert Tip

Depending on the level of expertise the book assumes on the part of the reader, the indexer may need anything from minimal to extensive knowledge of the language in question.

Dictionaries and Encyclopedias

Theological dictionaries, encyclopedias, and other types of reference work are a great place to start for indexers new to religious subject matter. Reference works provide a ready-made source for information, and of course are aimed at readers who want to find out more about a concept. They also divide into discrete, readily recognizable topics. However, these works tend to be quite long, and size is daunting when you're tackling a new knowledge base. Also, even introductory guides may make assumptions that can disturb the indexer. I recently talked with an indexer-friend from a Jewish background who was working on an encyclopedia of

Christian theology; she had real problems distinguishing what the authors meant when they referred to, for instance, "Hebrews." To a person from a Christian background it was clear even out of context that they were talking about the Epistle to the Hebrews, part of the Christian New Testament. Nevertheless, dictionaries and encyclopedias are a great place to start, either as a first religious indexing project or as a way to explore the subject matter. The Catholic Encyclopedia provides a great, free online source (http://www.newadvent.org/cathen) with detailed entries for persons, places, doctrines and so forth. A word of caution, however: Many religious groups use the same term in widely varied ways. The Catholic Encyclopedia, for instance, will give you a somewhat different slant on the concept of "sacrifice" than would a Protestant or Jewish or Muslim source. When relying on dictionaries and encyclopedias to aid your indexing of a text, make sure to match your project's belief system to the resource you are consulting, or try to consult multiple sources.

Children's Works

Children's books on religion make up an enormous market, but like children's books in other areas their simplicity is deceptive. Scholastic requirements and political sensitivities plant a minefield of difficulties for the novice. Indexers with experience in children's works probably make the best indexers of children's religious texts.

Biography/Hagiography

All religions have their "rock star" figures, and people have always thronged to hear their stories. The Gospels are at their root the story of Jesus' life, and the books of the Hebrew Bible (what Christians call the Old Testament) contain many biographies and biographical elements. Starting with Sakyamuni himself, narratives of saintly life have long been a staple of Buddhist literature. Hindu, Confucian, Muslim, and Shinto traditions all rely on hagiography, writings about holy people. Although Westerners tend to think of lives of medieval saints or of martyrologies when the topic arises, the tradition remains as strong today. Biographies of Billy Graham and Mother Theresa have been best sellers; "the Little Flower," St. Thérèse of Lisieux, died in 1897, yet multiple versions of her autobiography still sell briskly on Amazon.com. Biography is big business, and religious biography occupies a big corner of the market.

Biographies and hagiographies range from popular to scholarly, blandly admiring to cuttingly controversial. Saintly lives remain a staple of children's religious literature. Indexers of religious biography face the same issues dealt with in secular biographies. However, they also need to be aware of traditional structural elements in religious biography that readers will expect to find in the index. Conversion experiences, mystical awareness of the presence of God, and in Catholic and Buddhist biographies potentially miraculous occurrences, need to find their way into the index. Indexers should consult indexes to several biographies in the same tradition as their project. Hazel Bell's *Indexing Biographies and Other Stories of Human Lives* (Sheffield, England: Society of Indexers [UK], 2004) is a good general guide to indexing biographies; see also Martin White's excellent article on indexing biographies in Chapter 3 of this volume.

Feminist Theology and Liberation Theology

Feminist theology and liberation theology developed in the last 40 years. Feminist theology grew out of the women's movement and is heavily influenced by feminist schools of literary criticism and philosophy. Liberation theology is closely associated with Latin American religious and political thought; Marxist and socialist schools of historical and literary criticism also contributed ideas to this contemporary theological movement, which emphasizes Christian commitment to the poor. Within Roman Catholicism, its chief home, the Congregation for the Doctrine of the Faith *(Propaganda Fide)* criticized many aspects of liberation theology in two influential documents published in the 1980s; church disapproval, as well as the decline of Marxist-based intellectual theory after the fall of the Soviet Union in the 1990s, has greatly diminished the role of liberation theology. Recent surveys of theological trends barely acknowledge its existence. *The Oxford Companion to Christian Thought* (ed. Adrian Hastings et al., OUP, 2000) does not even contain an index listing for it. Nevertheless liberation theology remains a significant influence in Latin America, and both gay and black strains of liberation theology exist. Gustavo Gutierrez's *A Theology of Liberation: History, Politics, and Salvation* (Orbis Books, 1988) remains the classic text.

Feminist theological philosophy, on the other hand, remains a strong force in modern theological thought. Highly critical of the analytic school, feminist theology has helped to popularize interest in Continental philosophy among American and British scholars. It has also influenced many other theologies of the disaffected, including gay and black theories of religion, and liberation theology itself. Sarah Coakley's "Feminism and Analytic Philosophy of Religion" in *Oxford Handbook of Philosophy of Religion* (ed. William J. Wainwright, NY: OUP, 2005, pp. 494–525) provides an interesting introduction to the tension between feminism and analytic philosophy and theology. *The Cambridge Companion to Feminist Theology* (ed. Susan Frank Parsons, CUP, 2002) guides readers through the multifarious strands of feminist theology and its influences.

Legal Texts

The Abrahamic faiths (Judaism, Christianity, and Islam) all rely heavily on legal concepts and continue to produce many legal texts. The Muslim *Shari'a* is now a feature in our daily newspapers; the Roman Catholic Code of Canon Law affects the lives of millions of people around the world, especially as regards marriage. As for Judaism, many people will aver that Jewish belief and ritual practice *is* the practice of law. Indexers with a legal background often take to indexing theology with gusto. The various codes that govern Christian, Jewish, and Muslim society spawn the same sorts of periodically revised and updated regulatory addenda, case law, and commentary that secular law creates, and many of these texts need indexing. See my chapter on legal indexing in ASI's book, *Indexing Specialties: Scholarly Books* (Medford, NJ: Information Today, Inc., 2005) for an overview of indexing legal materials. Interested indexers may also want to look at the Canon Law Society of America's *New Commentary on the Code of Canon Law* (NY: Paulist Press, 2000) for an example of a legal theology project.

Comparative Religion

The field of comparative religion, the study of multiple religions and their common themes, had its inception with the discovery of the Americas. The priests who followed the conquistadors into Central and South America may have been repulsed by some of the religious practices they observed, but they were also fascinated, and some of them were able to see beyond their own religious traditions to shared commonalities. Concepts of natural law and human rights arose out of these early studies of non-Christian belief systems. Today comparative religion is an adjunct discipline of theology, philosophy, and anthropology. Indexers who enjoy working in those areas will also enjoy projects involving comparative religion. Huston Smith's *The World's Religions: Our Great Wisdom Traditions* (HarperSanFrancisco, 1991) is a classic of the genre. The works of both Mircea Eliade and Claude Levi-Strauss have greatly influenced the language used to talk about ideas across theologies, and indexers of comparative religion should find their writings helpful in choosing appropriate vocabulary.

Non-Western Religions

While works on non-Western religions may fall into any of the text types described in this article, the indexer may need to think about another sort of categorization entirely: texts directly out of the non-Western tradition, those written by Westerners, and those that attempt to amalgamate East-West concepts or apply non-Western religious ideas to our society and culture. Indexers need to be aware of these distinctions because they affect the way information is categorized. Different societies impose order upon thought in different ways. I once attended a university seminar on "Africa in the Middle Ages." The lecturer had to keep reminding us that the whole concept of the Medieval Period didn't really make sense applied to Africa. While, obviously, stuff was going on in Africa at the same time as stuff was going on in 11th-century Italy, it wasn't the same sort of stuff, and Euro-centric conceptualizations like "the rise of humanism" and "feudalism" just didn't apply. Western attempts to include non-Western cultures when writing generally about a topic can backfire, because the whole intellectual framework is the wrong shape.

Indexers can get caught between authorial intents and reader expectations. Readers of a translation of Hindu mystical writings, for instance, might expect to find the same sort of concepts in the index as they would in a European spiritual text, but those ideas just might not fit around the work in question. A Westerner writing about, say, Shamanism in Mongolia will have to adapt to concepts that the book's audience will understand while still reflecting the world written about, and the indexer must reflect both. A popular work on yoga might apply Chinese concepts of internal health and balance to thoroughly Western notions of stress. Simple awareness of the potential for cross-cultural messiness assists the indexer in producing coherent access to textual information. General guides to non-Western cultural concepts, such as *Buddhism: A Very Short Introduction,* by Damien Keown (OUP, 2000) also supply examples of content frameworks and key concepts that might otherwise get lost.

DEALING WITH DIVERSITY

Although I have attempted to be inclusive in my discussion of indexing theology, readers will certainly note a definite bias toward examples from Christian and Jewish works. This is hardly surprising, given my personal and academic background, but it does point up the issue of dealing with diversity when working with religious texts. We live in a world where a multicultural perspective is expected, but it can backfire on us. Authors with the best of intentions sometimes end up shoehorning traditions with which they are not entirely familiar into a framework that just doesn't fit, and indexers can fall into the same trap. Religion is so deeply embedded in our cultural processes that trying to work across traditions is fraught with difficulty. But none of us index because it's an easy job. Indexers love challenges, and theology certainly provides them. In that sense, it remains the queen of sciences.

Chapter 3

Indexing Lives

Martin L. White © 2005

"Human lives are generally not lived in accordance with strict principles, and irregularities in lives that are being indexed must be met with flexible indexing practice."
—Hazel Bell, *Indexing Biographies*

INTRODUCTION

Biographies are a species of monograph ("a written account of a single thing," *Merriam Webster's Collegiate Dictionary*), and they share many of the characteristics of other monographs. In what follows, I discuss some of the special problems that confront the indexer of a biography. For my purposes here, I include in the category biography not only accounts of one person's life by another person but also autobiographies and memoirs, studies of a period of a person's life (Lincoln's presidency, for example), diaries and journals, and even collections of a person's correspondence, as these genres often present similar problems for the indexer.

NAMES

Personal names create problems for the indexer in many types of indexing, but biographies present some problems of their own. Because many family members of the subject are often discussed, there may be many related individuals with the same surnames. The reader may not be able to keep all of the relationships straight, so I usually provide a parenthetical identifier stating the relationship to the subject, as in the following list from the biography of Elsie Clews Parsons:

> Clews, Henry (brother)
> Clews, Henry (father)
> Clews, Lucy Madison Worthington (mother)
> Clews, Robert (brother)
> Madison, Eliza Given (great-great-grandmother) [one citation; double-posted at Worthington]

31

Parsons, Dumesnil McIlvaine (mother-in-law)
Parsons, Elsie Clews
Parsons, Fanny Wickes (daughter-in-law)
Parsons, Herbert (husband)
Parsons, Herbert, Jr. (son)
Parsons, John (grandson)
Parsons, John (son)
Parsons, John Edward (father-in-law)
Parsons, Lissa (daughter). *See* Kennedy, Lissa Parsons
Parsons, Margot Worrall (daughter-in-law)
Parsons, McIlvaine (Mac) (son)
Parsons, Renée Oakman (daughter-in-law)
Parsons, Richard (grandson)
Worthington, Anna Tomlinson (grandmother)
Worthington, Edward (great-great-grandfather)
Worthington, Eliza Given Madison (great-great-grandmother) [one citation; double-posted at Madison]
Worthington, Frances Ann Slaughter (great-grandmother)
Worthington, John (great-grandfather)
Worthington, Lucy Madison (mother). *See* Clews, Lucy Madison Worthington
Worthington, William Hord (grandfather)

As the example indicates, there is often more than one individual with the same, or similar, given name. Parenthetical identifiers also aid the reader to sort out these entries. For women, a cross-reference from family name to married name (or the other way around, if the connection to the family name is stronger or more important than that to the married name) is perhaps even more vital than usual in order to have a listing for all family members at the family name.

A situation sometimes encountered in autobiographies and memoirs is that a relative will be mentioned merely as "Aunt Jane" or "Uncle John." If context permits inferring the surname with certainty, then the name can be indexed in usual surname-forename form; otherwise, "Jane, Aunt" or "John, Uncle" will have to suffice. The indexer might even want to consider entries for Aunt Jane or Uncle John.

With minor figures, the opposite case is also commonly encountered, that of someone mentioned with surname only, perhaps with a term of address (Mr., Miss, Capt., or Prof.). It might be argued that if the person is so minor that he or she isn't named in full, he or she doesn't merit an index entry. Only context can answer that question (and, generally, it's easier to justify including rather than excluding an item in an index). However, the name of the person involved in an event or anecdote may be the best way for the reader to retrieve the passage, even if the person is mentioned only by surname. If the indexer decides to include the name, some sort of identifying information should be provided in parentheses.

ENTRY FOR THE SUBJECT OF THE BIOGRAPHY
An Entry for the Metatopic?

Some people maintain that the metatopic should not have an index entry, because, after all, "everything in the book is about it." I would argue strenuously against this position for any book, but in the case of biographies, it would be disastrous. I believe that readers of biographies expect substantial index entries for the subject. Further, indexers usually provide them, as the following examples show.

The entry for the subject in the index occupies approximately:

- 17.8 percent of the total index to Anthony Cronin's biography of Samuel Beckett

- 10.7 percent of the total index to Martin Duberman's biography of Charles Francis Adams

- 6.8 percent of the total index to William McFeely's biography of Ulysses S. Grant

- 26.1 percent of the total index to Gerald Nicosia's biography of Jack Kerouac

- 14.55 percent of the total index to Howard Reich and William Gaines's biography of Jelly Roll Morton (the index is limited almost entirely to proper names)

- 10.29 percent of the total index to Bill Clinton's memoirs (or 16.57 percent counting the entries to which there are *see* references from the "Clinton, Bill" entry)

Of my own indexes to biographies, the entry for the subject in the index occupies approximately:

- 15.25 percent of the total index to Gerald Horne's biography of Shirley Graham Du Bois

- 11.8 percent of the total index to Desley Deacon's biography of Elsie Clews Parsons

- 16.5 percent of the total index to Allan Forsyth and Adam Hochschild's edition of the memoirs of Boris Sergievsky

- 6.8 percent of the total index to Vernon Snow's edition of the journals of Charles Snow (some of the information to Snow is posted at an entry "Snow, Charles, diaries," to which there is a cross-reference from the subject entry)

Expert Tip

The entry for the metatopic in a biography index is generally longer than that for the metatopic in a conceptual book. Periods, events, and characteristics common to most lives (childhood, death, family life) are the material of subheadings, not independent index entries.

Not all indexes to biographies have entries for the subject that occupy 5, 10, or 15 percent of the total. The entry for James Joyce in Richard Ellmann's biography occupies only about 2.4 percent of the total index, and in the same author's biography of Oscar Wilde, the entry for Wilde occupies only about 1.65 percent. The reduction is more apparent than real, however. In both indexes, all or most of the indexing to works is under the titles of the works (without much relationship established to the entry for the subject). If the works were included with their authors (as is done in the Nicosia biography of Kerouac, for example), the percentage for the subject entry would be considerably higher. (I'll return to the questions of relating authors and their works later.) Another reason the subject entries are so much smaller in the Ellmann biographies is that much of the indexing is distributed to other entries ("eyesight" and "Italian language" for Joyce, for example, and "trials" for Wilde) without cross-referencing from the entries for Joyce and Wilde, which seems a significant omission. Finally, the subject entries for both of these biographies contain subheads with long strings of unanalyzed locators; analysis would have lengthened, as well as improved, both indexes considerably.

General Concepts vs. Singulars

The entry for the subject of the biography is probably the greatest problem that confronts the indexer. In most monographs, the metatopic is a general concept (African-American literary theory, diplomatic immunity, particle detectors, prime-time television programs, to mention a few from my experience). General terms can be analyzed into their species and proper parts, as in a thesaurus. Such narrower terms will generally bear a great portion of the indexing so that the buildup of citations will occur at their entries, not at that for the metatopic. The entry for the metatopic might consist largely of subheadings referring to chapters or major sections, and a *see also* cross-reference to the narrower terms. In the case of prime-time television, the bulk of the indexing is likely to be under the types of program (situation comedy, police drama, medical drama, westerns) and particular programs, rather than at the entry for "prime-time television programs."

Even in indexes to works of history, which, like biographies, are concerned with singulars rather than general concepts, the metatopic can usually be analyzed into proper parts, which will carry most of the indexing. A war, for example, can be broken down into campaigns, battles, and generals, and most of the indexing will occur at those entries rather than at "Civil War" or "World War II." As with general concepts, those entries will often contain only indexing to chapters or major sections and a *see also* reference to the campaigns, battles, and generals.

Human lives, unlike general concepts and historical events, are not easily analyzable into species and proper parts. There are periods, events, and characteristics common to most lives (childhood, death, family life), but those are the material of subheadings, not independent index entries. For this reason the entry for the metatopic in biography indexes is generally longer than that for the metatopic that is a general concept.

ANALYSIS AND LOCATOR STRINGS

It doesn't appear to me that the problem of long locator strings is different for biographies than for other genres; however, as discussed previously, human lives, being singulars, aren't amenable to being parsed into sets of narrower terms, leading to a large buildup of locators at the subject entry. Yet there are techniques to analyze strings without exceeding the number of subhead levels allowed. For example, in the Clinton memoirs, under the first-level subheading "President: Second Term" there are 16 unanalyzed locators at the second-level subheading "arms control and," 12 unanalyzed locators at the second-level subheading "initiatives and proposals of," and 13 unanalyzed locators at the second-level subheading "nuclear proliferation and." As the index allows only two levels of subheadings, no further analysis is possible at the Clinton entry. However, if "arms control," "initiatives and proposals," and "nuclear proliferation" were made index entries, they could be analyzed. *See* references could then be created from the corresponding subheading at the Clinton entry:

> Clinton, Bill
>> President: Second Term
>>> arms control, *see* arms control

This move would have the benefits of analyzing long strings of locators and creating entries for "arms control," "initiatives and proposals," and "nuclear proliferation," which are not entries in the actual index. The Clinton index uses this technique in other instances (such as the elections of 1992 and 1996), so it would not be a departure from the format used. This technique only works with terms that can be considered "look-ups." You might well decide that "achievements" (nine locators) can't stand alone as an index entry. Even "initiatives and proposals" could be questioned as an independent entry.

Hazel Bell, in Chapter 10 of the book *Indexing Biographies,* discusses a number of techniques for reducing long unanalyzed strings of locators for other characters in a biography and justifications for allowing them. Space and time considerations aside, I would treat locator strings in biographies as in any other genre: analyze them when they exceed a certain minimum (some publishers set a minimum number, in fact).

ORGANIZATION OF THE SUBJECT ENTRY
Organizational Subheadings

The organization of the subject entry is probably the most discussed topic in biography indexing. Much of that discussion concerns whether the subheadings should be arranged alphabetically or chronologically. However, there is a prior question that needs to be considered that will bear on the alphabetical/chronological debate.

In my opinion, a single level of subheadings is inadequate for the large entry for the subject that almost always occurs in biography indexes. The first question regarding the organization of the subject entry is that of a system of first-level subheadings under which the subheads can be organized (which I call organizational headings or grouping headings). Hazel Bell addresses this question in Chapter 9 of *Indexing Biographies*. Among the examples she gives are (bibliographical information appears in *Indexing Biographies*):

> Jane Austen: Adult life; Relationships; Writings (the latter including Letters, Novels, and Verses) (p. 35)

> Richard Burton (the actor): Career; Characteristics and Tastes; Acting; Wealth; Relationships; Marriages; Writings (p. 35)

> Winston Churchill: Characteristics; Education; Finances; Health; Hobbies; Military Career; Political Interests (p. 35)

> Bertrand Russell: Biography; Characteristics; Attitudes; Beliefs and Pleasures; Writings (p. 36)

Among the biographies just mentioned, the following systems appear (in the order in which they occur in the index):

> Charles Francis Adams: Personal Life; Professional Career; Scholarly and Literary Pursuits

> Samuel Beckett: Ailments; Death; Early Life; Female Friendships; Literary Life; Male Friendships; Marriage; Sexuality; Social Life; War and Post-war Years; Works (subdivided by genre); in addition

there are many subheads (some of broad significance, others very specific) that have no dependent sub-subheadings.

Bill Clinton: After an alphabetically-arranged series of subheads pertaining to miscellaneous characteristics and activities (for example, "campaign style of"; "musical interests of"; religious interests and activities of"), there are five chronologically arranged organizational subheads: Childhood and Early Youth; Higher Education, Political Apprenticeship; Governor of Arkansas; President: First Term (1992–1996); and President: Second Term (1996–2000). The latter are in boldface type with title capitalization.

From my own indexes come the following systems (subheadings in italics have no dependent sub-subheadings):

Becker, Jurek
    awards and honors for
    books and stories of
    friendships of
    and Jewishness
    and language
    in Lodz, 1937–39
    in new Germany, 1989–97
    in opposition in GDR, 1974–78
    personal characteristics of
    political and social views of
    relationships with women
    as scriptwriter in GDR, 1960–74
    sources for opinions of
    in Soviet zone, 1945–49
    in United States
    in West Berlin, 1978–89
    during World War II
    as writer
    as young communist in GDR, 1949–60

Franklin, Benjamin
    and American Revolution
    as businessman
    early life in Boston
    educational projects of
    education of

birth of
during the Civil War
death of
diaries of. *See* Snow, Charles, diaries
education of
in 1868
family life of
at fifty
financial difficulties of
health of
in LaSalle, Illinois
in Ottawa, Illinois
personal habits of
in Peru, Illinois
political activities of
in Pulaski, New York
religious life of
social life of
in temperance movement
weather conditions affecting
working life of

It's clear that my organization lacks the economy of the indexes noted by Bell and especially of the index to Duberman's biography of Charles Francis Adams, which has only three organizational headings for 1 1/2 page index entry. I'm not sure that that is such a bad thing. If the material lends itself to being sorted into a handful of categories, then that handful serves adequately. My experience finds that a handful of categories is rarely enough. Aspects of the life or career of the subject that are mentioned often (the FBI surveillance of Shirley Graham Du Bois, the health of Elsie Clews Parsons, or the leadership qualities of Jacob Schiff, for example) usually become organizational subheads in my indexes. Sometimes such groups can be fairly easily combined, other times not. One is confronted by something like the old opposition between precision and recall here. The fewer the organizational subheads, the more likely that distinguishable pieces of information are lumped together; the more precise the organizational subheads, the more difficult it becomes to navigate the entry to find what one is seeking. As in most of my indexing decisions, I choose to err on the side of precision, and generally my mostly academic clients seem to prefer it.

Since my subject entries tend toward a larger number of organizational headings, I do not create a system of organizational headings as I index.[1] Rather, I wait until I've finished the indexing and have done a provisional edit of all the other entries before addressing the issue of organizing the subject entry. Of course, during the indexing process, I will probably see certain categories developing, and I may make a few notes to that effect, but I find it more efficient to wait until I have all of the indexing in place before attempting its organization.

The subheads for the subject of the biography fall into two major categories: those citing the chapters or major sections of the book and those citing particular facts about the subject. Those citing chapters or major sections will usually, of course, have a number of second-level headings subordinate to them as well. In the index for the biography of East German Jewish filmmaker Jurek Becker, the following organizational headings refer to entire chapters:

> in Lodz, 1937–39
> in new Germany, 1989–97
> in opposition in GDR, 1974–78
> as scriptwriter in GDR, 1960–74
> in Soviet zone, 1945–49
> in West Berlin, 1978–89
> during World War II
> as young communist in GDR, 1949–60

Each of these eight subheads refers to one of the eight chapters of the book. Not all biographies are so well behaved, especially those that have a topical rather than strictly chronological organization, of which the Franklin book (which wasn't a strict biography as its theme was the Americanization of Franklin) is an example. The other organizational headings, "relationships with women" and "in the United States," for example, group references to Becker's various marriages and love affairs and to trips to the United States that are mentioned in different chapters pertaining to the various periods of his life. The heading "books and stories of" contains subordinate headings pertaining to his prose works, while "as scriptwriter in GDR, 1960–74" contains those to his employment and works as a scriptwriter in East Germany.

Expert Tip

My strategy is to wait until I have all of the indexing in place before attempting its organization. The subheads for the subject of the biography will fall into two major categories: those citing the chapters or major sections of the book and those citing particular facts about the subject.

As I noted above, the organizational subheadings are usually suggested by the subheadings that have come up during indexing, as well as from chapter titles and other major text headings. Depending on the activities of the subject of the biography, organizational subheadings such as "early life," "education," "family life," "personal characteristics," or "views of" almost force themselves on the indexer.

As the subjects of many of the biographies that I've indexed are writers of one sort or another, most of my indexes have an organizational subheading "works." In my experience, authors of biographies are quite concerned to make sure that I'll relate an author to his or her works. At a "works" subheading, I'll duplicate all of the works that have no subheadings and provide a *see also* cross-reference to those works that do.

Subheadings pertaining to the relationships of the subject to other people usually are grouped under "family life" or "marriage" (for family relationships) or a grouping subheading pertaining to an activity such as "political activity" (for political activities) or "business life" (for business activities). As can be seen above, however, sometimes a grouping heading "friendships" is useful. In the Shirley Graham Du Bois index, the relationship of the subject to her husband, W. E. B. Du Bois, was so significant that it required a separate subheading. Often, with personal relationships the references are exactly the same at the entries for both the subject and the other person. Generally, I duplicate them at both places, but if space is an issue (as it was, for example, in the Benjamin Franklin book), I'll make a *see* cross-reference from the subject to the entry for the other person.

I try to discipline myself to include no singleton subheads in the entry for the subject, that is, first-level subheadings with no subordinates. Occasionally it happens that there is a subheading for a chapter or major text section (what would ordinarily be an organizational subheading) without any subordinate sub-subheadings. A biography might have a short chapter on the childhood of the subject with no other mentions of childhood events in other chapters. In such a case, I would not consider it especially problematic to leave the heading in without subordinates. In the examples here, "sources for opinions of" from the Jurek Becker biography and "documentation of life of" from the Elsie Clews Parsons biography (both from the introduction) are singletons of this type. I do consider it problematic to leave in a singleton that should clearly be a sub-subheading (in that it is of smaller scope than the grouping subheadings), but for which there are no other similar entries to group it with. The existence of such a subhead will often spur me to return to the text to find similar references to group with it, which often improves the index. If that fails, I'll try to shoehorn the lone subheading into one of the existing grouping headings (sometimes generalizing the grouping heading to include the new reference). If all else fails, I might delete the offending subhead on the grounds that it's just too detailed for the index. The reader may note that the entry for Charles Snow (previously mentioned) contained quite a few singleton subheads. This is because the book was not a biography, but an episodic journal with editorial introductions between sections that had numerous instances of single references to important information (birth, death, etc.).

Format and Typography for Organizational Subheadings

The publisher determines most issues of format and typography, but there are things that the indexer can suggest that will make navigating the index, especially the entry for the subject, easier. As stated earlier, I don't think it's possible to create an entry for the subject without at least two levels of subheadings. However, many academic and trade publishers require paragraph (run-in) style indexes. Although there are techniques for displaying two levels of subheadings in a paragraph-style index (see, for example, the 14th edition of the *Chicago Manual of Style,* section 17.146, they are so visually complicated that I would never recommend them. If the publisher can't be persuaded to accept a fully indented entry for the subject entry, the combined indented and run-in style (with the first-level subheads indented under the entry word and the second-level subheads run into the first-level subheads paragraph style) is a good compromise. The first-level subheads are given visual prominence by being indented, but the look and feel, as well as the space-saving characteristic, of the paragraph-style index is maintained (see section 17.146 of the 14th edition, or sections 18.27 and 18.28 of the 15th edition, of the *Chicago Manual of Style* for examples).

The use of special typography to emphasize first-level subheads can aid the user. I find that preceding each first-level subhead with an em dash is sufficient, but others prefer using italic type or caps and small caps for first-level subheads.

Alphabetical vs. Chronological Ordering of Subheadings

The question of whether the subheadings in a biography index (I limit myself here to subheadings for the subject entry) should be organized alphabetically or chronologically is one of the most debated topics of biography indexing. The situation is more complicated than that, however, as Hazel Bell points out. Bell gives four orderings for subheadings in a biography: page, chronological, alphabetical, and thematic/classificatory. By thematic/classifactory, she means subsuming the subheadings under general headings that I've called organizational headings in the preceding section. As I don't think that the index to any serious biography can do without organizational headings, in my view Bell's thematic/classificatory approach is always required. But the problem remains, how should the organizational headings be arranged, and how should the subordinate subheadings be arranged under the organizational headings?

First, the arrangement of organizational headings. In my experience, organizational headings are so general that no chronological order could be assigned to all of them ("education," "marriage," and "later life" perhaps, but not "personal characteristics," "works," and "views"). Page order is no more applicable than chronological. I usually fall back on alphabetical order, as everyone understands it (if they understand any order at all) and it's what a reader expects in an index. Bell, who, as we have seen, prefers indexes with fewer organizational headings than I find feasible, suggests a combination of alphabetical and chronological orders. In an entry that, among others, has headings for World War I, World War II, the Korean War, the Vietnam War, and the Gulf War, you might consider leaving them in that order rather than alphabetizing them. Doing so, however, presupposes that the user knows the chronology of those wars. While most users know the chronological order of 20th-century wars, they might not know that, in the biography of an academic, for example, the subject taught at Xavier, Cornell, Southern California, and Duke, in that order. Unless there's strong reason to do otherwise, I stick with alphabetical order of organizational headings.

Second, the arrangement of subordinate, second-level subheadings. Here the options are page order, chronological order, and alphabetical order, as we've already grouped these subheadings thematically. If the narrative follows strict chronological order (which in my experience, is rarely, if ever, the case), page and chronological orders will be equivalent, or close to it. When page order and chronological order are not (roughly) equivalent, it's difficult to conceive of any benefit to using page order. How is the user to divine how the author has structured the narrative? Further, as Hazel Bell points out, page order is generally maintained only for the first locator for each subhead; whatever benefit there might be to page order is lost if there is more than one locator per subhead.

Third, the chronological arrangement. I've already alluded to the benefit of using chronological ordering of subheads: Most users understand the chronology of a human life and will look higher up in the string for primary education than for marriage and children. Of course, the user may not know the chronological order of many events in the subject's life, such as marriages to different spouses, professional appointments, or journeys. Further, creating such an order requires that the indexer know the exact chronological sequence of every reference. This isn't very difficult if the narrative is arranged strictly chronologically or if the author always provides exact dates for each topic. Rarely are these conditions met. Bell points out another problem with chronological arrangement, when, for example, "someone's personal appearance at various states of their life; repeated visits to the same place" have to be separated chronologically rather than grouped together.

Last, the alphabetic order for arrangement. The principal benefit of alphabetical arrangement of subheads is clear: everyone can be assumed to understand it (discounting secondary questions of numerals and special characters). The principal defect seems equally clear: The user has to know what word he or she is looking for. In many cases things will be clear: Look in the E's for "education," in the M's for "marriage," and so on. This presumes that the user can anticipate what term the indexer has chosen, and that that term appears in filing position ("in front," as we say). Clearly, these conditions are not always met. Subheads can always be framed in different ways, and all indexers know the difficulty of forcing the key word "in front."

So, to sum up, which is it—page order, chronological order, or alphabetical order? Unless the narrative is strictly chronological, page order has little to recommend it. Both chronological order and alphabetical order have an intuitive appeal, but both present problems to both indexer and user. In my experience as an index user, I find that I'm more frustrated by chronological than by alphabetical arrangement. That may in part reflect my experience as an indexer; I can't say whether nonindexers have the same response. But I do think that, unless the client requests chronological arrangement, or there's clear reason in the text for using it, it's hard to go wrong with the good old ABCs.

ENDNOTE

1. If I read the text through before I began indexing, as Hazel Bell strongly recommends in her chapter "First Read Your Book," I would doubtless have a greater idea of what the system of organizational headings would be before creating the first entry, but even that would be only provisional and I'd be cautious about committing too much work to a scheme that wasn't final.

REFERENCES

Brown, Scot. *Fighting for US: Maulana Karenga, the US Organization, and Black Cultural Nationalism.* New York: New York University Press, 2003.

Cronin, Anthony. *Samuel Beckett: The Last Modernist.* New York: Harper Collins, 1996.

Clinton, Bill. *My Life.* New York: Alfred A. Knopf, 2004.

Cohen, Naomi W. *Jacob H. Schiff: A Study in American Jewish Leadership.* Hanover, NH: Brandeis University Press, 1999.

Deacon, Desley. *Elsie Clews Parsons: Inventing Modern Life.* Chicago: University of Chicago Press, 1997.

Duberman, Martin B. *Charles Francis Adams, 1807–1886.* Boston: Houghton Mifflin, 1961.

Ellmann, Richard. *James Joyce.* New and revised edition. Oxford, UK: Oxford University Press, 1982.

Ellmann, Richard. *Oscar Wilde.* New York: Alfred A. Knopf, 1988.

Gilman, Sander L. *Jurek Becker: A Life in Five Worlds.* Chicago: University of Chicago Press, 2003.

Horne, Gerald. *Race Woman: The Lives of Shirley Graham Du Bois.* New York: New York University Press, 2000.

McFeely, William S. *Grant: A Biography.* New York: W. W. Norton & Company, 1981.

Nicosia, Gerald. *Memory Babe: A Critical Biography of Jack Kerouac.* Berkeley, CA: Grove Press, 1983.

Reich, Howard, and William Gaines. *Jelly's Blues: The Life, Music, and Redemption of Jelly Roll Morton.* Cambridge, MA: Da Capo Press, 2003.

Sergievsky, Boris. *Airplanes, Women, and Song: Memoirs of a Fighter Ace, Test Pilot, and Adventurer.* Edited by Allan Forsyth and Adam Hochschild. Syracuse, NY: Syracuse University Press, 1998.

Snow, Vernon F. *A Child of Toil: The Life of Charles Snow, 1831–1889.* Syracuse, NY: Syracuse University Press, 1999.

Wood, Gordon F. *The Americanization of Benjamin Franklin.* New York: Penguin, 2004.

FOR FURTHER READING

Bell, Hazel. *Indexing Biographies and Other Stories of Human Lives.* 2nd edition. London: Society of Indexers, 1998.

——. "Indexing Biographies: Lives Do Bring Their Problems." *The Indexer*. Vol. 16, No. 3, pp. 168–72.

——. "Indexing Biographies: The Main Character." *The Indexer*. Vol. 17, No. 1, pp. 43–44.

Knight, Norman. *Indexing, the Art of.* London: Allen & Unwin, 1979.

Walker, Alan. *Biographical Indexing* (review of Hazel Bell's *Indexing Biographies*). Available at http://www.aussi.org/anl/archive1999-2001.htm

Wellisch, Hans. *Indexing from A to Z.* 2nd edition. New York: H. W. Wilson, 1995.

Chapter 4

Indexing Encyclopedias

Marion Lerner-Levine © 2005

This article is based on my experience working in-house at *Collier's Encyclopedia* (the full title is *Collier's Encyclopedia with Bibliography and Index),* a general encyclopedia of 24 volumes, including the index volume, aimed at readers from high school through college and beyond. The thorough scope and literary quality of this encyclopedia, however, made it an excellent reference source for literate adults and older students, as well. For about six months each year, from 1989 through 1996, I worked on the annual update and revision of the encyclopedia. Rose Bernal, the head indexer who hired me for the job, was my mentor and supervisor. When Rose retired, her successors Mary Humphrey and Nila Glikun supervised the conversion to computerization, working with David Ream, consultant from Leverage Technologies who converted the printed index to a database using Indexing Research's CINDEX program, professional version.[1]

When I first arrived, we were still using index cards. Our indexing method with the cards is described under "Cross-References" and "Mechanics of Indexing," later in this chapter. Although detailed and time-consuming, and involving many more steps than computer indexing, this method actually lent itself to well-thought-out concepts and subtle fine-tuning. There was an enormous bank of file cabinets containing approximately 200,000 index cards organized by volume and page number. Not long after, in 1994–95, the encyclopedia was computerized. In 1996, Collier's editorial staff was working on a CD-ROM prototype, and was incorporating the paper index into it, so the index card files disappeared along with our library of invaluable ancient and dog-eared reference books.[2] After being bought out by a succession of international publishing groups in the late 1990s, Collier ceased paper publication.

SELECTION CRITERIA FOR ENCYCLOPEDIA INDEXING

When indexing encyclopedias, use the following criteria:

- *Persons* – Applicability and enhancement of the article text should be considered in order to warrant an entry. The nationality and the field of accomplishment should be given in parentheses as an identifier after the heading. Examples: **DUNCAN, ISADORA** (Amer. Dancer); **DUMAS, ALEXANDRE** (Dumas père) (Fr. Au).

- *Places* – More than one specific fact should be given; location alone is usually not enough to warrant an entry. However, scattered references on one page would justify an entry for what would otherwise seem to be scanty information.

- *Things* – Almost all explained terminology, whether scientific, sociological, artistic, and so on, is usually indexed; events such as battles, treaties, and so on, should be indexed if the text includes more than allusions to them; and names of specific things should be indexed if they are definite, definable, and give the answer to a specific, intelligent question.

Expert Tip

Unless there is a substantial piece of information about the person, do not index the name.

INDEXING PRACTICES

Supervision and Coordination

If possible, one person should be in charge of the work and should go over the work of the other indexers. This is necessary in order to maintain a tight control over the terms used for headings and subheadings. Whether the indexing is done on cards or with the computer, the head indexer supervises, making sure that the spellings are correct and that the locators are written accurately.

Method

The indexer should keep in mind that the purpose of the index is to help the reader to locate quickly the information that he is seeking. A consistent, methodical approach is required. This holds true whether you are establishing rules for a new index or updating and revising an old one. If new, determine the style and scope, taking into account the amount of space, time, and user access required. Follow the rules as scrupulously as possible, but deviate from them when it seems necessary. Allowing for a style that is adaptable to later revision will make it easier. If the encyclopedia to be indexed is a revision of an older work, the new index entries must be styled and alphabetized to fit in with the old index. But if the encyclopedia is a new one, decisions about the index style and alphabetization of entries should be made before the work is begun. The order and style of the index entries must follow the order and style of the article titles in the encyclopedia. Questions to ask are: Will article titles and therefore index entries be alphabetized letter-by-letter or word-by-word? Should entries that are article titles be printed in boldface all caps? Should all names beginning with "M," "Mc," or "Mac" be alphabetized as if they were all spelled "Mac"? Should entries beginning with "St." be alphabetized as if spelled Saint? Must all headings have identifiers?

The same good indexing practices that apply to the indexing of books with single authors also apply to the indexing of books with multiple authors; but works with multiple authors, especially works that are to be revised at regular intervals, are trickier to index than books with single authors. The indexer must be familiar with the terminology of various fields to ensure that information is not scattered under several synonymous headings. For example, Southern writers often call the Civil War battles the *Battles of Manassas*, while Northern writers call them the *Battles of Bull Run*. Follow the author's terminology whenever possible, but if there is a discrepancy among the authors, consult the editors of the encyclopedia and consult other reference books to determine the preferred term. If there is a choice, use the more popular or the more common term, and make a *see* cross-reference from the term not used. Internet searches can be extremely useful to determine the commonly accepted term.

When indexing a specific article, it is not always possible to ascertain whether the same information is available elsewhere; but material that the indexer is certain exists in another article may be omitted. For example, in an article on a town, the name of a famous person who was born there might be mentioned. Unless there is a substantial piece of information about the person, do not index the name—the article on the person will surely give his birthplace. When indexing a country or a state, important cities need not be indexed if the encyclopedia contains entries on the cities. Of course, if there is a long discussion of the history of the city or of important events that took place there, the city should be indexed. In making new entries, beware of having duplicate headings—and never make double entries. This is called *double posting*, which usually is not allowed in the indexing of works that are to be revised and updated periodically. Check for entries under alternative headings or synonyms, different spellings, or inverted or compound headings, and use *see* cross-references to avoid scattering information under synonymous headings. While double entries might be correct for one edition of the encyclopedia, they can lead to problems in subsequent editions. Assume, for example, that there is no article on Mark Twain, but that he is discussed in depth in the article on AMERICAN LITERATURE, and that instead of making a cross-reference from Samuel Clemens to Mark Twain, the indexer gives the page reference under both names. In a later edition the article SHORT STORY might use only the name Twain in an account of his work, and the indexer might index that name only. The page reference would be entered under Twain, but not under Clemens because the indexer did not know that there was an entry under the other name. Similarly, if the person who indexes the article DENGUE makes two entries—

one for dengue and another for break-bone fever—the person who indexes the article on EPIDEMICS and sees a discussion of break-bone fever might not realize that it is also called *dengue*, and would index it under break-bone fever only.

Abbreviations

If abbreviations are to be used in the identifications for entries, a list of acceptable abbreviations is drawn up, and they are printed in the usage notes at the beginning of the index. Only abbreviations on the list can be used. The usage notes should also include the alphabetization system and the ordering of entries.

Example of abbreviations list:

> **orient.** oriental
> **pros.** prosody
> **trans.** translation, translator
> **SS.** saints
> **St.** saint

HEADINGS

Every article title in the encyclopedia should be a main heading in the index. In *Collier's Encyclopedia*, the index headings that were article titles were printed in boldface capitals, volume numbers were set in bold face, and page numbers in light face. Index headings made from material within the article should be as precise and concise as possible. The common or more familiar term is generally chosen and a cross-reference made from the technical or more esoteric term. Ideas and concepts not specifically mentioned in the text may be used as headings when they are clearly implied. Index only definite, definable subjects, and do not index mere mention of names, places, or events.

Expert Tip

Always index under the more specific heading. For example, <u>*wood carving*</u> *would be indexed under the heading "decorative arts," not under the more encompassing heading "art."*

Singular or Plural Headings

In deciding whether to use the singular or the plural form of a heading, the preferred encyclopedia style for headings is the singular, which actually has a more universal and inclusive connotation than the plural. The article title, which is generally a singular term, governs in choosing the entry heading. This is in contrast to back-of-the-book indexing style in single-subject reference and scholarly books. In that context, headings in either the plural or the singular may be indicative of more specific connotations that are treated in the texts of these books. Exceptions to the "singular" rule could be the use of entries such as COMMUNITIES, COOPERATIVE as well as COMMUNITY (concept of), INDUSTRIAL RELATIONS, and peoples, such as COMANCHES or DISSENTERS. In a yearbook, the plural form is more often used because the yearbook is concerned with specific events of a specific year, such as Earthquakes, Hurricanes, or Fires.

The encyclopedia also makes use of categorical subheads followed by specific sub-subheadings.

Example:

WORLD WAR I
--Armaments
    flame throwers
    gas mask
--Battles
    Argonne
    Verdun
--Economic and Sociological Aspects
    black Americans
    conscientious objectors
--International Diplomacy
    Central Powers
    Fourteen Points
    freedom of the seas

Inverted Headings

Headings are inverted in order to place the keyword first. Although there is no question about the necessity of inverting such headings as BLIND, EDUCATION OF THE, other cases, such as Electric circuit and Circuit, electric, are not so easily decided. In considering whether to invert a heading, try to determine which element of the heading a searcher would be most likely to look for first, and make a cross-reference from the heading that was not chosen to the heading that was used.

Compound Headings

Compound headings such as COLLEGES AND UNIVERSITIES are used for terms that are so closely related that they cannot readily be separated. A cross-reference

would be made from <u>Universities</u> to the heading, which is the article title: COL-
LEGES AND UNIVERSITIES.

Self-Indexing

Ordinarily, entries from within the article should not be entered as subheads under
the same article title in the index—this is called *self-indexing*. For example, an article on Robert E. Lee will contain a discussion of the Battle of Gettysburg. Do not
list <u>Gettysburg, Battle of</u> with the page number where it is discussed in the Robert
E. Lee article under the heading LEE, ROBERT E. There will most likely be an article on GETTYSBURG, BATTLE OF, and this title should be entered as a subhead
under LEE, ROBERT E. <u>Lee, Robert E.</u> can be entered as a subhead under the heading GETTYSBURG, BATTLE OF. Note that the often-used convention of using
"and" or "at" (for instance "GETTYSBURG, BATTLE OF <u>Lee, Robert E.</u> at") as
part of a subhead entry is not generally used in encyclopedia indexing.

The exception to the self-indexing rule is in the indexing of very lengthy articles,
especially "country" articles such as Italy where there are subdivisions such as —
economic resources, — education, — ethnology, — finance, — geography — government, — social and cultural life. References from the main article are placed as
the first blind references before references from other articles. Subdivisions cross-
referenced to other headings that may or may not be article titles include — History:
see Italian history, — Language: *see* Italian language.

Assuming that there is no article on the Cuban missile crisis, the article on United
States history would be expected to contain a discussion of it. To help the reader who
is searching for information about U.S. foreign relations under the index entry
UNITED STATES HISTORY, and who might not recall this specific incident, the
subhead <u>Cuban missile crisis</u> can be entered under UNITED STATES HISTORY —
Foreign Relations with the page number where it appears in the UNITED STATES
HISTORY article. Of course, <u>Cuban missile crisis</u> must have its own entry in the
index. Most other articles are indexed in the conventional way, that is, the pickups
in the text are added to other headings in the index, or new headings created. A thesaurus, or authority list of pre-existing headings in the encyclopedia, should be
referred to before a new heading is created.

Page Ranges

It is not necessary to give a range of pages for a heading that is an article title or
a side head in an article; the page number on which the title or side head appears is
sufficient. A range of pages may be given, especially for entries from long articles,
when the reader might not otherwise be able to determine that the discussion continues on succeeding pages.

Identifiers

In a general encyclopedia, names of persons should be identified by nationality and position or field of endeavor (English king, American biologist, and the like). Persons of the same name and nationality or profession can be distinguished by using birth and death dates. Names of places and physical features should be identified by place (country, state, or province). Terms used in a specific discipline should be identified by the field (mathematics, biology, literature, etc.). Only abbreviations on the master list, previously described, should be used.

Indexing Names

Ancient and medieval personal names and names from non-Western languages can be a problem for the indexer. Should the name be inverted? Should the article precede the name? Should a noble be indexed under his name or under his title? No hard and fast rule can be made; each case must be considered separately. Consult other reference works and consult the editor of the article. If discrepancies among the articles are found, bring them to the attention of the editors. [3]

There are often changes in geographic names, in medical and scientific terminology, and even in names of persons (from Cassius Clay to Muhammad Ali, for example). Newer articles will use the most recent name or term; but older articles, or articles written from a historical perspective, might use the older name or term. For example, a discussion of British colonial history might call the country now known as *Zimbabwe* by its name during the colonial period, *Southern Rhodesia*. Of course, there will be a cross-reference from <u>Rhodesia</u> (form. S. Rhodesia) to <u>Zimbabwe</u>; but to make sure that the reader who consults the articles listed as subheadings under ZIMBABWE and who comes across the old name will know that he is reading about the history of Zimbabwe, the old name can be placed in parentheses following the heading: ZIMBABWE (form. S. Rhodesia). Another example would be <u>Mordvinians</u> (Mordovans) (people). For the same reason, pseudonyms should be included in headings when appropriate; however, when the pseudonym is more well-known, the connection is treated thus: Saki (Munro, Hector Hugh (Br. au.); Munro, Hector Hugh (Br. au.) *see* Saki. In this instance because Saki is the more commonly known name of this author, a cross-reference from Munro, Hector Hugh (Br. au.) would be made. *Collier's* style was in general not to enclose the pseudonym in parentheses.

The heading of terms that are not article titles should be as precise and concise as possible. Do not index mere mention of names, places, or events. However, as mentioned earlier, scattered references on one page might justify an entry for what would otherwise be scanty information. Books and paintings would be indexed as main heads only if there was an article devoted to them, such as GONE WITH THE WIND (nov., Mitchell) or NIGHTWATCH (paint., Rembrandt). But, for example, if in the article on Flaubert there was a lengthy analysis of his novel *Madame Bovary* it would be indexed as **Madame Bovary** (nov., Flaubert).

SUBHEADINGS

While the heading of an entry is of a general or comprehensive nature, the subheadings underneath it are used to direct the searcher to more specific or related information on the subject. Do not enter long strings of locators (called blind references) without a subhead; and do not use a subhead for a particular type of information one time and then make a blind reference under the same heading for a similar piece of information. For example, under the heading PORTER, WILLIAM SIDNEY, a reference to <u>Short Story</u> (general information) can be entered without a subhead, but references to two of his most famous stories (specific information), assuming there are articles on both of them, should *both* be entered with a subhead: *Gift of the Magi* and *Ransom of Red Chief.* Don't use a subhead for the title of one story and not use it for the title of the other.

The subhead is most often the title of the article from which the information is taken, as in the example, but when a word or phrase other than the article title would give a better indication of what the text covers, it should be used. For example, the article UNITED STATES discusses the defense policy of John F. Kennedy. The subhead <u>United States</u> under the heading KENNEDY, JOHN F. would prove much too general. In this case the subhead <u>defense policy</u> gives a clearer idea of what the text actually covers. In another example, the article on ALLOYS, would probably discuss brass, bronze, German silver, and other specific alloys. Under the heading METALS, do not list each alloy that is mentioned in the article; instead list only the article title <u>Alloys</u>. An interested reader will go to the ALLOYS article. If he is seeking more information, he will look in the index for the specific alloys mentioned in the article.

Except in rare instances, only the volume and page number(s) from one article should follow the subhead. For example, in indexing <u>Isabella</u> under Spanish history, give only the reference to the article ISABELLA (Sp. q.). If the searcher is especially interested in Isabella he will look her up in the index under her own heading and find many other references.

An exception might be made in an entry such as HAN (Chinese dynas.), in which two references could be given after the subhead <u>sculpture</u>; one reference from the article <u>Sculpture</u> and another from the article <u>China</u> in which there might be a substantial discussion of the sculpture of the Han dynasty. It would look like this (note that volume number is in bold):

Han (Chin.dynas.)
    sculpture **6**-35; **20**-75

In general, practice consistency, and when considering new subheads look at the entry to see how the subhead would fit under it. For example if indexing an article on the actor <u>Alfred Lunt</u>, do not automatically list him under the heading American drama. If you look at that entry you will notice that there are no other actors' names listed under it. Either make the list complete by listing all the actors and dramatists under the heading, or do not list anyone under it.

Posting Up

Many entries will be picked up from long articles, of course, but try to pick up at least one entry from short articles—this nails down the article and categorizes it. Index the article under the next broader heading or the more specific heading. Blank verse should be indexed under Poetry, not under Literature; Poetry should be indexed under Literature. Similarly, ladybird should be indexed under BEETLE, not under INSECT. Beetle should be indexed under INSECT. This is called posting up. Make sure that the list is complete. If scarab and tumblebug are listed under BEETLE, but ladybird is not listed, the reader might assume that there is no article on the ladybird. If the list generated by posting up becomes too long and unmanageable, the subheads in the list can be deleted and replaced by a general *see also* cross-reference: BEETLE, *see also* names of specific beetles.

CROSS-REFERENCES

Since the articles will be written by many different authors with varied backgrounds and will be read by subscribers of different ages, backgrounds, and educational levels, be generous in the use of cross-references. This is especially important when indexing encyclopedias that will be undergo periodic updating. An older subscriber might know the disease *poliomyelitis* by its once common name of *infantile paralysis*. A cross-reference can alert him to the change in usage and send him to the place where the information will be found. The indexer should try to keep informed about these changes in terminology.

See cross-references are made from synonyms, from the second part of an inverted heading (Korea, North, *see* North Korea), or sometimes from an exact opposite (Illiteracy, *see* Literacy). *See also* cross-references are used to direct the reader to related information: MEDICINE, *see also* specific diseases; VIETNAM HISTORY, *see also* Vietnam War.

Be alert to changes in personal names (such as Muhammad Ali from Cassius Clay) and to changes in geographic names (such as Leningrad and Saint Petersburg). Divorced people in the news take cross-references from former names to current, or vice-versa if the person is better known under the former name. Jacqueline Kennedy Onassis comes to mind. She is generally thought of as Jacqueline Kennedy. If there were an article on her under Kennedy, all the more reason to keep her there, as article titles govern.

When indexing *Collier's Encyclopedia*, we sometimes found very long lists in the index and had to consider whether they were necessary. There was a long list of countries under Gross domestic product. We considered replacing this list with a few general page references under Industrial production and a cross-reference *see also articles on specific countries.* Each article on a country included a discussion of the economy and the gross domestic product.

Verification of the Index Cross-References

The very last operation before the index is printed is the verification of the cross-references. Before the introduction of computer-assisted indexing, this was done by having a verification file alphabetized by the term to which the cross-reference referred: Bull Run, Battles of from Manassas, Battles of; Potato tree from Mullein nightshade; Cambodia from Kampuchea; Ceylon from Sri Lanka. The index cards in the verification file provided a permanent archive of the changes to cross-references. Whenever a new cross-reference was entered on the old galleys, a new card was made for the verification file. The indexer, using galleys of the index on which changes had been made, would check each heading that had been deleted or changed against the verification file and would delete or change the cross-reference accordingly. Indexing software can now do this job quickly and can make a list of cross-references that are no longer valid so that the indexer can make the appropriate changes or deletions.

Cross-References in the Text

Editors and authors often make cross-references in the text of the encyclopedia because they feel that a reader familiar with a particular term will look it up in the text without consulting the index. Therefore every cross-reference in the text (Manassas, Battles of, *see* Bull Run, Battles of) should be a cross-reference or a direct reference in the index. While cross-references in the index direct the reader to index entries where the information may be found, cross-references in the text direct the reader to the articles themselves. In the Civil War example given here, a cross-reference in the text sends the reader to the article title that is synonymous with the name of the battle he is looking for, and a *see* cross-reference is necessary for the index. However, a cross-reference in the text might read, Particle accelerator, *see* Physics. This would not be an appropriate cross-reference for the index because the terms are not synonymous; rather, the indexer should go to the article on Physics and make an entry for Particle accelerator with a direct reference to the page where the information on particle accelerators may be found. Another example could be a text cross-reference Strip mining, *see* Coal mining. For the index, a direct reference to strip mining should be picked up from the article on coal mining.

ALPHABETIZATION

Entries in the index should follow the same alphabetical scheme used for the article titles in the text. This will generally be in the conventional order of persons, places, and things.

Headings for persons with the same name are usually listed with saints first, followed by popes (and antipopes) and rulers. Names of more ordinary persons are listed next, and are distinguished by prenames, nationality, occupation, and, if necessary, by birth and death dates. In computer-assisted indexing, codes are used to force the headings to fall into the proper order. During the computer conversion of *Collier's* index some disorder was introduced into this conventional hierarchical arrangement. Overcoding of these names led to some strange arrangements, and we had to hand-tweak them to make the names sort properly.

Examples: Henry, Saint
Henry I (English king)
Henry VIII (English king)
Henry I (French king)
Henry IV (French king)
Henry, Joseph (American scientist)
Henry, O. (American writer)
Henry, Illinois
Henry (electrical measurement)

Stevenson, Adlai Ewing (American politician; 1835-1914)
Stevenson, Adlai Ewing (American politician; 1900-1965)

Nicholas, Saint
Nicholas I (pope)
Nicholas V (pope)
Nicholas V (antipope)
Nicholas I (Russian emperor)

ILLUSTRATIONS, MAPS, AND BIBLIOGRAPHIC REFERENCES

Illustrations should be indexed from the caption only—if the term is not printed in the caption, don't try to guess what the illustration is. A picture of a particular bird might look like a whippoorwill to the indexer when in reality it is a nighthawk. If an illustration is deleted from an article, delete its listing only, and not the entry heading.

Guides to the maps for countries and states will generally list many small towns and many physical features of lesser importance. In general, only the most important towns and features should be indexed. Index from the guides, not from the maps themselves.

In *Collier's*, but not in all encyclopedias, the bibliography was accessible from the index. (*See* Kister, endnote #4.) Bibliographic articles are listed as subheads, below the main subheads and after maps and illustrations.

Examples:
> **Commedia dell'Arte**, **7**-59; **1**-93 etc. (volume number in boldface; page number in lightface)
>> pantomime
>> ___*Ill*. **1**-93
>> ___*Bib*. **24**-75: *1-414*

> **Coma Berenice** (astron.)
>> cluster **10**-542
>> ___*Ill*. **10**-535
>> ___*Maps* **21**-488,489
>> ___*Bib*. **24**-141: *85*

MECHANICS OF INDEXING

In pre-computer days, an index card was typed for each entry in the index, with only one page number per card. The cards were filed in page number order, and the file might contain more than 200,000 cards. When an encyclopedia page was revised, the cards for that page were removed from the file. As the new page was indexed, entries for which there were cards were underlined on the page in blue, let's say, and the necessary changes were marked on the cards; or, if the entry was no longer valid, the cards were marked <u>delete</u>. New entries were underlined on the page in red and new cards were typed for them. The changed, new, and deleted cards were alphabetized, and the changes, deletions, and additions were entered on galleys of the previous index. The cards, including cards for which there were no changes, were then sorted in page order and returned to the file. The deleted cards were thrown out. Records of pages worked on were logged in to show what pages had been handled. At Collier's, revisions were indexed from copy folders of updated text and manuscripts of new articles were fitted into space created by deleted and amended text. The pages were divided into quadrants, 4 quads per page: 17a, 17b, 17c, 17d, for instance. This involved painstaking work in that many revised and new cards had to be placed in a verification file because the indexers couldn't tell if run-overs to following pages or columns would involve a change of quad as well as a page change. These cards were later checked and the quads verified on page proofs. Sometimes last-minute changes in the articles led to inaccuracies in page references at the tops and bottoms of pages and columns. Quad indexing was done away with at the onset of computerization.

The computer took over much of the tedious work, and a new method of indexing was developed when index cards were discontinued. Indexers worked from page proofs of the articles as before. Separate computer files for each letter of the alphabet were pulled out from the complete index in Volume 24 of *Collier's Encyclopedia*. After all of the changes, revisions, and additions to each file's index had been incorporated, the separate indexes were merged back into the final volume. The completed index was proofread intensively, through many passes, since this process could lend itself to the creeping in of new errors.

Just as happened in card indexing, errors in location numbers and spelling were found by the vigilant index supervisor. Some examples of detected errors and mis-spellings were: "Chichen Itza" indexed as "Chicken Itza," and "Woman in White" (novel) as "Women in White." "Rosetta Stone" was inverted as "Stone, Rosetta," a lake or river located in two states was listed twice (Cumberland River, Ky. and Cumberland River, Tenn.) when it should have appeared only once with a double-state location (Cumberland River, Ky.- Tenn.), and "Lima, Peru" illustrations were entered under "Lima, Ohio"! An encyclopedia indexer should have an unusually broad scope of general knowledge and a keen eye to find and eliminate such errors before publication.

SUMMARY OF PROCEDURE

Before beginning to index a new encyclopedia, a list of all the articles should be given to the indexer. If the work is a revised edition of an old encyclopedia, the indexer should be provided with a list of all the pages that are to be revised. As she receives articles and pages to index, she can check them off her list to make sure that she sees all the changes and additions. The indexer should be given her own copy of the new and edited pages so that she can underline them or make notations of what she is picking up in the margins. These marked-up pages should be kept in page order so that, if necessary, they can be referred to during the preparation of the new edition or in the preparation of future editions.

Sometimes the editors will assume that a text page does not have sufficient changes to warrant providing the indexer with a copy of the new page. This is often the case, especially if only a death date is being added to a biography or a population figure is being updated. However, editors sometimes miss other changes that have been made to the page and are often not attuned to indexing; what seems minor to them might be important to the index, and only the indexer can judge this rightly. The indexer should be given a copy of *every* page that is revised.

When indexing with the computer, the indexer, as mentioned, should use her own copy of the pages to index. For a revised work, the computer can generate a print-out of the entries that were previously indexed from a specific page so that she can compare the entries with the new copy. Using the printout, she can underline in blue, say, any entries indexed in the old copy that are still valid; she can underline or write in red any new entries that she wishes to make, and on the printout she can mark any entries that she wishes to delete or change. She should then input these new entries, changes, and deletions in the computer. She should make a printout of the new entries, and give that along with the printout of the old entries and the copy from which she worked to the chief indexer to be checked and corrected. The checked and corrected pages should be returned to the indexer so that she can see where she went wrong and make the necessary changes in the computer.

Last of all, before the index is sent to the printer, the cross-references should be verified. The indexer's marked-up pages should be filed in page order and kept, maybe for years, until the next revision of the page. Page proofs of the new index should be returned to the indexer for proofreading. Last minute changes are made, running heads are checked, widows are eliminated, and anything that mars the appearance of the index is corrected.

REFERENCE MATERIALS FOR THE ENCYCLOPEDIA INDEXER

Editors on the staff of the encyclopedia are an important resource. The editors at *Collier's Encyclopedia* were experts in specialized fields with extensive, in-depth knowledge in their respective scholarly areas. Even if an editor knows little about the technique of indexing, he may be able to resolve perplexing problems of spellings of names, scientific nomenclature, and the like, that often confront indexers, and he may direct questions to the author or authors.

The indexer should have her own copy of the general English-language dictionary favored by the publisher of the encyclopedia. It is also useful to have access to the unabridged giant desk-stand *Webster's* to refer to when a rare or unusual word needs definition. Specialized dictionaries, such as *Merriam Webster's Biographical Dictionary* and *Merriam Webster's Geographical Dictionary*, are useful. There are also dictionaries and encyclopedias of art, music, philosophy, law, religion, sports, science and technology, and so on, that can be consulted when needed. *The World Almanac* and *Facts on File* are useful for checking current names and events. The indexers at Collier's used the *Encyclopaedia Britannica* and the *Encyclopedia Americana*, as familiar and reliable sources of information. Nancy C. Mulvany's *Indexing Books* and Hans H. Wellisch's *Indexing from A to Z* provide useful guidance on the practice and technique of indexing. The ASI (American Society of Indexers) Web site has excellent lists of other resources and Web sites. Nancy Mulvany's *I-Torque* newsletter is a must-read for reference and Web site information. Catalogs from Information Today, Inc. (http://www.infotoday.com), among others, list many useful book titles. Internet discussion groups such as *Index-L*[5] provide an additional resource.

ACKNOWLEDGMENTS

Many thanks to Rose Bernal, former head indexer of *Collier's Encyclopedia* and to freelance indexer Vitrude DeSpain, who was my colleague at Collier's and previously an indexer for *Encyclopedia Americana*. They were most helpful to me on the writing of this article. They contributed practical notes on the creation and editing of the index, rules of alphabetization, types of headings and subheadings, typefaces, methods of working, and methods for clarification of information. In addition, they looked over the manuscript and made suggestions for its improvement.

ENDNOTES

1. Ream, David, "Encyclopedia Sorting Rules," *Key Words*, ASI Newsletter, Vol. 5, No. 1, Jan./Feb., 1997.
2. The advent of the multimedia encyclopedia on CD-ROM and on the Web has changed things. Indexing of encyclopedias in these electronic formats is done differently, and involves embedded indexing and detailed search capability. However, conventional indexing and analytical skills are still needed in order to keep the utility and accessibility of the resulting indexes. An interesting interview with Kenneth F. Kister in *PubZine.com* on the Web describes the impact of the new technologies on the encyclopedia marketplace.
3. See "Online Resources for Foreign Names" compiled by Sue Nedrow, in *Key Words,* Vol. 11, No. 4, Oct.–Dec. 2003, pp. 106–109.
4. *See* Kister, Kenneth F., *Kister's Best Encyclopedias: A Comprehensive Guide to General and Specialized Encyclopedias*, 2nd Edition, Oryx Press, 1994, pp. 25–26, which includes a discussion on Broad Entry (*Collier's*) compared with specific entry (*Encyclopedia Americana*) encyclopedias. He reveals, also, that in the 1994 editions the ratios of index entries to text words was 1:50 in *Collier's*, 1:90 in *Britannica*, and 1:90 in *Americana*.
5. Freelancers who are indexing large subject encyclopedias for commercial publishers will find information in the *Index-L* archives, including an interesting discussion between Katharyn Dunham and Martin Tulic on estimates and billing for such projects on *Index-L*, Wednesday, April 10, 2002.

Chapter 5

Indexing Art Books and Catalogs

Susan DeRenne Coerr © 2005

When a museum visitor, I supposed that the art objects on view that day would stay put in the galleries just where I saw them. Later, when a museum staffer, I learned that the works of art and object labels are changed quite often, and that every collection object has a record documenting its own "career."

Time-lapse photography of a gallery would reveal various objects or their labels "appearing and disappearing" from view. A curator might reorganize gallery themes and object groupings, retiring some pieces to storage and retrieving others to go on view upstairs. Individual collection items are taken off display to go behind the scenes for collection management reasons such as photography or examination in conservation laboratories. Some objects travel away in custom-fitted crates while out on loan to temporary exhibitions at other museums. So art objects are presented to us in new combinations often, either physically (on view in new or special exhibitions), or by images assembled in new books.

Before I describe indexing art books and catalogs, I will discuss the various types of art publications, and then review the categories of information collected about individual artworks and material culture objects (physical objects produced by a society or culturally cohesive group).

Expert Tip

There are "art books" about art, there are "artist's books," and art is used to illustrate books.

WHAT IS AN "ART BOOK"?

There are different contexts for art images in publications. Sometimes art object reproductions, photographs, or drawings may be included in a book mainly as *illustrations* to accompany the text. For example, a textbook on American history may include museum-owned images, such as the gelatin silver photographs taken by Arnold Genthe during the San Francisco earthquake and fire of 1906. (Genthe's work can be found at the Fine Arts Museums of San Francisco site: http://www.thinker.org/index.asp.)

Artists' books are unique individual art objects that *look* like books. They are sculptures or book-like assemblages that artists make to explore some of the visual and physical features of books, but these works of art do not communicate in the ways characteristic of books, and usually they do not need or have indexes.

BOOKS ABOUT ART, ARTISTS, AND ART HISTORY

Indexes are needed when a *book is about art images*, and has a text discussing and even comparing them. For groups (of artists or of objects), common characteristics are described, and variations on themes are analyzed. Common cultural origins or object uses are also discussed. In a *monograph*, the career growth of one artist may be traced over time, with examples from various types of media.

Historical contexts influence the creating, collecting, and survival of specific works and classes of art.[1] For example, a dramatic historical overview of perilous art object journeys during wartime is the 1994 prize-winning book *The Rape of Europa: The Fate of Europe's Treasures in the Third Reich and the Second World War,* by Lynn H. Nicholas (*see* References).

The subject of this chapter is books about works of art and aspects of indexing these books. Appearances in art books and art catalogs become part of an art object's history and the index should help the reader or researcher locate specific objects in the publication. A good introduction to this field by Marilyn Rowland and Diane Brenner appeared in *Indexing Specialties: History,* "Indexing Art and Art History Materials," a 1998 ASI (American Society of Indexers) book.

Various examples of types of art publications that are indexed are referenced in the Endnotes at the end of this chapter. There are scholarly and popular books, monographs on an influential artwork[2] or one individual artist, surveys of groups of artists,[3] media studies (such as books on intaglio prints, 19th-century French furniture,[4] or Japanese kimonos[5]), and period studies (on the Bauhaus, or the commissioning of Chinese and Tibetan art during the Qing[6] dynasty).

There are also various types of art catalogs: gallery or museum exhibition catalogs,[7] permanent collection catalogs of museum holdings,[8] and auction house catalogs. Other art world publications are histories of personal collections,[9] museum periodicals (newsletters, journals, and board minutes), and art organization histories or newsletters.[10] (Museum publications such as education pamphlets, gallery brochures, and building maps usually don't include indexes.)

After I review some of the typical categories of information kept on individual art objects, I will discuss some aspects of art book indexing. (*See* "Indexing Art Publications" later in the chapter.)

ART OBJECT INFORMATION CATEGORIES

The "Careers" of Art Objects

Art objects and historic artifacts (objects made, modified, or used by humans) that are collected by public museums or private collectors all have their own life histories. Every object in an organized collection has its own record or file that is updated whenever new information becomes available. The object information categories available for one object may be minimal, as on a person's tombstone (or better, as on someone's periodically updated driver's license), or extensive, as on the résumé of a person who has attended several schools and held a number of jobs.

The following artist and art object information categories are some of the most common that are preserved in owner records and discussed in art publications that need indexes. "Art objects" may be assigned to fine art categories or be examples of folk art, tribal pieces, or historic artifacts from ancient civilizations, specific societies, or formally constituted nations. Information is derived not only from the physical characteristics of each object, but also from historic facts compiled on the *provenance* (previous ownership) and "career" activities of the art object. Not all the categories of information I describe below are known for every object, nor are all included in every art book.

Object Origin Information

Origin information includes the *personal names* of the artist, designer, or maker, with the life dates of each, and sometimes alternate attribution names. Geographical origin data may include the continent, country, province, village, tribe, or culture where the maker lived, and the time period or historical era during which the object was created.

Other personal names may be on record, such as those of family members, teachers, artist collaborators, artist assistants, apprentices, or artisans who worked with the artist. There may be names of people who the artist did not know personally, such as engravers or photographers who "reproduced" images of an artwork.

If an author uses *one-word artist names* (Caravaggio, Picasso), a useful online resource for determining full names and the alphabetization of compound names is the Union List of Artist Names (ULAN) maintained by the Getty Research Institute in Los Angeles, California. The preferred name in ULAN is the name used most often in scholarly literature among other known names. It is generally the form of the name in the language of the artist, called the "vernacular" name (indicated in bold in their examples). It is also the indexing form of the name; that is, it is listed in inverted order with the last name first, if there is a "last" name (go to:

http://www.getty.edu/research/conducting_research/vocabularies/ulan). Choosing which categories of personal names should be included in the index depends on the depth of discussion of the various groups of people, and the space and budget allotted for the index. For example, if space is tight, the indexer might include only other artists, immediate members of the artist's family, and perhaps important patrons of the artist, but *not* include the names of nonartists, nor artwork donors whose names are seen in book illustration captions.

Other object origin information may include *names of institutions* relevant to the artist's career, such as schools the artist attended or taught at and the names of awards or fellowships won by the artist. Sometimes there is the name of a studio, workshop, foundry, or factory that was involved in the fabrication of the artwork. Included in the scope of ULAN are "corporate bodies" that are creators of art or architecture. Examples are legally incorporated bodies (such as architectural firms) and other groups of people working together to collectively create art (e.g., the *Gobelins Manufactory* of tapestries, or the *Della Robbia* family).

Art Object Identification Information

Each object has a *name* (type of object) and sometimes a formal *title* as well. It is a convention that the indexer uses the terms presented in the publication being indexed, and avoids arbitrarily naming the objects seen in the images. Care should be taken when choosing between singular or plural object names for a heading or subheading. For instance, the AAT Thesaurus uses both forms but the museum community generally prefers descriptors in the singular (Bella Hass Weinberg, p. 98, *see* References).

The *date* the object was created is often given. There may be only a final date, or a number of previous dates when an art image has evolved over time (such as fine print states, preliminary drawings and sketches, earlier models or casts of a sculpture). There may be alternate versions of the image in other media (such as a full-color oil painting image that has been translated or "copied" as a black-and-white print). If there is no specific date known (*n.d.*), or no approximate date (*circa, ca., c.*), the object may be assigned to a period in art history, for example, the Renaissance, or Depression Modern.

If *titles* of art objects are to be indexed, a consistent format should be chosen. This involves consideration of indexing full or truncated titles, and whether to include alternate titles (such as those in another language, or earlier assigned titles). It should be decided whether the index headings for titles of artworks are to be placed beneath the artist's name, or whether they should appear as individual headings (perhaps with the artist's name or initials added as a qualifying phrase), or both. In a monograph, the featured artist's own works could be indexed directly under their titles, whereas works by all other artists in the same book might be placed only under those artists' names.

If the book discusses an artist's writings or books as well as his or her art, a special treatment may be needed to distinguish literary works from artworks. The literature titles could be followed by the artist's last name or a tag with the artist's initials, for example, (KK) for Käthe Kollwitz. The publication title could be given in bold instead of italics or have an explanatory phrase added, such as (book) or (article). (The categories represented by variations in typeface formats should be explained in the index introduction.) Sometimes an artwork has a nickname, which *might* be indexed, but only if it is discussed in the text. For instance I've heard art history students refer fondly to the famous painting *The Birth of Venus* (by Sandro Botticelli, c.1480) using a title you would *not* index, "Venus on the half-shell." (Just for fun, a good book of cartoons that are witty and often anachronistic visual variations, not title takeoffs, after well-known Western European fine art masterpieces is *Art Mafterpieces*, by Ward Kimball. *See* References.)

The indexing of a book with many artworks captioned "Untitled" poses a special challenge. (*See* "Indexing Untitled Works of Art" later in the chapter.)

Medium and Material

The *medium* and *material* are common visual object data categories. Examples are cast sculpture, oil painting, wood furniture, hard paste porcelain, assemblage, and samplers (needlework embroideries made by women or girls to demonstrate skill with a variety of stitches). Object *dimensions* and sometimes the *weight* (in pounds or kilos), are often on record. In the art world, dimensions may be given in inches or centimeters (or both), usually in order by height, width, then depth. The inner and outer dimensions of a mat or frame may be on record, or the size of a sculpture base or pedestal, especially when the artist who created the work designed the frame or base. An art book may include an indexable discussion of dimensions, such as when there is an analysis of scale, or of some art objects now physically separate, which originally may have been together in a unified larger whole.

Sometimes when writing an index, a *heading clarification phrase* can be added to *homographs* (words with the same spelling but different meanings) to distinguish among them. For example, if the following identical or similar words with different meanings were in the same index, there could be qualifiers added in parentheses to differentiate the headings:

> cartoons (newspaper)
> cartoons (Renaissance fresco)
> cartoons (tapestry)
> frames (period picture)
> frames (of reference)
> frames (web page)
> media (commercial communications)

media (fine art)
medium (paint base)

Types of Images

If an artist uses a variety of media, and the number of examples is small, the indexer may want to index a group of objects of like media together.

An art book may contain reproductions of mass-produced media such as posters, postcards, or art exhibition flyers. Since art photography media proliferated in the 20th century, art object images may be reproduced in black-and-white or color, and in single-frame views such as film or video stills, or digital images. The artists' own lifetime photographs may be part of the art, as documents of performances or conceptual works, or scholars may have had posthumous images (estate prints) made from the artist's negatives. (*See* examples under "Indexing Untitled Works of Art" later in this chapter.)

History of An Object

Provenance information (a record of previous ownership or previous locations of a work) may include owner names and geographic locations or the ownership date-spans of patrons (royalty; individuals; foundations), and architectural commissions. The Getty Thesaurus of Geographic Names (TGN) online site focuses on places important for the study of art and architecture (*see* References). *Institutional names* may be related to the history of an individual object. These names include foundations commissioning or collecting an artwork, art galleries or museums where it was exhibited, and citations for the names of libraries or historical societies holding relevant records.

Nonmaker labels on the objects may have come from previous owners, framers, art dealers, customs offices, or institutional borrowers (such as exhibition title labels). The *literature* or *references* for an art object may come from writings by the artist, books that the artist read, experts and literary figures quoted in the text, museum journals, exhibition reviews, and mentions or reproductions in other art history books.

Confidential Information

Owners of art objects also maintain *confidential information* about art objects. This type of information is rarely published unless it is old enough to have become part of the historic record. The private data can include appraisals or evaluations, insurance values, purchase records, lender or vendor contact information, physical condition reports, x-rays and condition photographs, and storage location. Records for fragile or extremely rare objects may have annotations regarding special handling, display, or storage restrictions, and travel requirements or limitations.

Object Descriptions

Art objects may be described from various viewpoints, sometimes while neglecting the other perspectives. A *fabrication summary* may discuss the materials of which the object is made, the medium, the support (canvas, paper, wood panel), and the techniques used to make it. This type of description may include the location and text of the maker's signature, a date, or other inscriptions. Sometimes there are symbols or trademarks on the object, such as maker marks, a designer or factory logo, or a watermark in the paper.

The *intended use* of an object may influence the type of description and the assignment of the object to a curatorial department in a museum. For example, an artist's work in glass could be considered a container (decorative arts), or a sculpture (fine arts).[11] A tribal object might be described mainly in connection with its use in specific cultural ceremonies.

A *recognition description* answers questions like these: What does the object look like? What are the dominant colors and shapes? Which decorative motifs are prominent? Does the artwork depict religious, mythological, or historic events, or other recognizable subject matter? Are there iconographic symbols? A description in words may have been recorded when there was no visual image or reproduction available.

If several different styles are presented in the art book, the index could have headings for discussions of these terms. Art style names may be identified by period, (Quattrocento; Turn of the Century), by groups of artists contemporary to each other (Futurists; the School of …), or by style names assigned by later scholars (Mannerism, Postimpressionism).

If more information on an art style or period discussed in an art book text is needed, the indexer can search the Internet for "art history resources on the Web" and find sites with many links, such as "The Mother of All Art and Art History Links Page" at the University of Michigan (http://www.art-design.umich.edu/mother), and Chris Witcombe's site at Sweet Briar College (Virginia), "Art History Resources on the Web" (http://www.witcombe.sbc.edu/ARTHLinks.html).

Art Object Identification Numbers

There are numbers assigned by the artist or maker, such as a date or chronological identification number shown near the artist's signature, and edition numbers (for objects in series, such as original prints, photographs, or cast sculptures).

Museums or other organized collections may have assigned an object number that is sometimes included in art book image captions. It is interesting to note that *museum numbering systems* are unique to each institution and that they are *not* used for cataloging objects into art categories, as is done by librarians using Library of Congress or Dewey decimal systems for books and publications.

Instead, museum numbers are used for identification (when looked up in museum records or databases), and for tracking. Every museum receipt, objects list, or internal location transfer order will include a number matching each piece. To facilitate inventories, some museums use bar-code numbers (on object labels and tags, storage room doors, shelves, containers, and even personnel identification badges.) The identification and location bar codes are linked to the museum object numbers in the collection database.

Museum object numbers usually signify ownership status (permanent collection or loan) and the year of entry into the specific institution, and they have varying quantities of digits. Sometimes accession numbers are subdivided into group and even part numbers (for entire donor collections, or for components of a set). In the latter case, one section of a complex museum number may be applied to all the components of a silver chocolate service, or of a nomad's yurt (a circular tent-like structure with skins or felt stretched over a collapsible lattice framework), or the multilayered trays of useful implements and equipment included in a French *necessaire* (military campaign travel case). The last component of an object number might be a unique letter for each physically separate part that belongs together with another part, such as *a* and *b* to identify a matching cup and saucer set.

Museum identification numbers are often given in art book image captions, but usually they are *not* included in an index, unless the publication is a comprehensive collection catalog. For example, a two-volume history and inventory of 1,905 buildings in the Presidio of San Francisco forts[12] had five indexes: "General Index [including canons and other armaments], Names Index [personal names], Military Units and Organizations Index, Building Index by Name, and Building and Structure Index by Number."

Computerized Art Information

There are a variety of different *software programs* in use for museum databases, collections information management systems, and publicly available museum Web sites, however not all museums are computerized. There is no unified national database of art objects in U.S. public collections, whereas the Canadian Heritage Information Network site (http://www.chin.gc.ca/English) is a publicly accessible national inventory.

The Museum Computer Network (http://www.mcn.edu) is one of the online sites that provide news of museum computerization programs in the U.S. Recently the printed Bulletin of the American Society for Information Science and Technology (ASIS&T) featured a special section of 28 pages on Museum Informatics, including an article on "Tools and Methods for Leading End-Users to Collection Information" (*see* References). There are online databases of commercial photographs and images (for advertisers, graphic designers, publishers, and multimedia producers). One such site is named Index Stock Imagery (http://www.indexstock.com), which has a keywords list (but not an actual index).

Art and art information using Internet capabilities sometimes appears exclusively online. An intriguing site showcasing art collections and collectibles viewable only on the Internet was noted by Nancy Mulvany in the June 2004 issue of her *i-TORQUE* online journal: The Museum of Online Museums (MoOM) is at http://coudal.com/moom.php. There are other sites showcasing digital art being created only online using keywords and free association approaches with the image-retrieval capabilities of popular search engines like Google. These pieces are literal and virtual "found art"! (*See* Mirapaul.)

Art Publication Object Numbers

Within art publications, various types of numbers may be assigned to the objects. These numbers include catalog numbers or temporary exhibition checklist numbers, plate numbers, figure numbers for illustrations or graphics on text pages, and sometimes references to catalog raisonné numbers. (A complete, systematically arranged list of all the known works by an artist, compiled by an expert scholar, is a catalog raisonné. Another type of catalog raisonné is a complete list of items from a specific cultural site, such as all the excavated gardens and patio flower boxes inventoried in Pompeii.[13])

An *index heading note* at the top of the index should explain the different types of numbers from the book that are used in it. Sometimes this can get quite complex, for example:

> Italic numbers refer to pages where illustrations appear; figure numbers are not cited in the index. Roman numbers refer to the Color Plates. Spalliera paintings are included by title, by cycle title, and under artist names, along with checklist numbers in square brackets. The locations of spalliera paintings in both Renaissance and contemporary collections are listed by the names of the palazzi, museums, or collections and are followed by checklist numbers and italic page numbers where the paintings are illustrated.[14]

INDEXING ART PUBLICATIONS

During the initial review of the art manuscript to be indexed, the indexer makes sure that the client has included the table of contents, captions or a list of the illustrations, and all the illustrated images. (Sometimes graphics or art plates arrive from a different printer or production house than the one sending the text.)

Level of Detail to Be Indexed

The indexer of an art publication needs to consider the content and emphasis of the publication, and choose just enough of the information given for objects presented in the book to create index headings, which

- include every object illustrated;
- include nonillustrated objects, if they receive substantial text discussion or are in a checklist to be indexed;

- differentiate like objects from each other;

- reflect relationships among objects;

- reflect terms and concepts the audiences of the publication will expect to find indexed.

The indexer should discuss these considerations with the client (the editor and/or the book author), so that the breadth of coverage and the depth of the index are cooperatively determined. This planning should be done before indexing starts, in order to reach agreement on such important factors as the publication space (pages) allotted for the index, the time needed for indexing, and, of course, the indexing budget.

The Author's Knowledge vs. the Indexer's Knowledge

When an author is involved in index planning, natural tensions can arise between the indexer and the author. The author usually knows the subject matter and the book itself, while the indexer knows the art of indexing and how to create a new auxiliary document to supplement the book text and provide the reader with an important information tool. In her review of the Getty Research Institute *Guide to Indexing and Cataloging with the Art & Architecture Thesaurus*, Weinberg notes (p. 100), "A curator may do the description while a cataloger [or indexer] selects the access points because [quoting from the Guide]: 'The knowledge required to describe and analyze an object is different from the expertise necessary to index the object.' " (See References.)

There may be tension also between the amount of art history detail in the book and the goal of economy in indexing. The scholar's research may reflect years of work and carefully assembled facts, yet not all the information presented in the book may fit in or even belong in the index. For example, it is important to agree on whether the people names, artwork titles, or terms provided in the footnotes should be indexed. And sometimes the information in the book appendices may be too detailed to index, for reasons such as limitations on the index space (pages) or the indexing budget.

Expert Tip

There should be agreement between indexer and client on what is to be and __not__ to be indexed in each different part of an art book.

How Much Should Be Indexed?

A common method indexers use to estimate index size is to determine the number of indexable pages in a publication, and then calculate the *average index entries per book page* appropriate for an index that is thorough but not exhaustive and reasonable but not too expensive.

However, many art books have pages that look so different from one another that the appropriate quantity of index headings per page can vary widely. There may be some pages with only a single plate and caption, and text pages either with or without captioned figures. Appendices might contain a detailed checklist, a chronology, a list of exhibitions, an artist's concordance, a compilation of contemporary press exhibition reviews or other literature citations. The indexer may analyze and discuss with the client both the categories and the quantities of indexable names and topics, which are typical of each of the different types of pages in the book. There must be agreement on what is to be and *not* to be indexed in the different parts of an art book.

Follow-up indexing work may be expected if the client wants the opportunity of reviewing the initial index, making suggestions, and even asking for revisions. Once the index file with feedback is returned, the indexer may make changes, edit the index into an integrated whole once again, and then produce a final version. When any such open-ended index review or iteration phases are being planned, the indexer and client may decide that the indexing work estimate should be on an hourly fee basis instead of a page rate.

Capturing Captions

The backbone of an art book index is information from the image captions. The indexer and publisher need to agree on which categories of caption components should appear in the index and which should not.

Expert Tip

Caption information is the backbone of an art book index.

The most common art object data elements that may be found in captions include name of artist (or school), original title, translated title, date (or period), medium, and dimensions. Useful lists of typical information categories for various media are given by Hans Wellisch in his 1995 book *Indexing from A to Z*. He also discusses approaches to indexing NPM (nonprint materials), that is, physically separate objects that have been assembled into stored and displayed collections (*see* References).

Organization of Art Titles in an Index

In an art history survey book, or a general art catalog[15] covering many different artists, the titles of their artworks are generally placed in alphabetical (or sometimes chronological) order as subentries under the artists' names. Usually there isn't enough space also to index the titles individually (i.e., double-post them). However, the indexer may make some exceptions and index certain individual works by their titles to assist the readers. The next pair of entries include a cross-reference made from an object title or nickname that may be better known than the name of the creator:

> Fur teacup and saucer and spoon, Surrealist. *See* Oppenheim, Meret
> Oppenheim, Meret, *Breakfast in Fur* (1936), 200, *201*

Or, individual pieces might be indexed because the *subjects* of the artworks are famous:

> Goodridge, Sarah, *Daniel Webster*, 66, *67*
> Huntington, Daniel, *Daniel Webster and Washington Irving*, 80, *81*
> Irving, Washington, with Daniel Webster, drawing by Daniel Huntington,
>   80, *81*
> Webster, Daniel,
>   portrait by Sarah Goodridge, 66, *67*
>   with Washington Irving, drawing by Daniel Huntington, 80, *81*

Indexing Related or Duplicate Art Titles

There may be works of art that are closely related to other artworks, by either the same artist or other artists. Sometimes there is a chronological relationship between two works, when one is a preliminary drawing or study for another, or the artist has created a work "after" (modeled on) an earlier work. These works may or may not have identical titles. The following index entries exhibit these relationships (in this case, boldface numbers indicate pages on which illustrations appear):

> Cassatt, Mary,
>   *Evening,* preparatory drawing (1879/80), 104, **105**
>   *Evening,* etching and aquatint (1879/80), 104, 106-107, **106**

> Hassam, Childe, *Weir's Garden,* 126, **127** [a watercolor of the same
>   garden spot is seen in another entry, for a related work by the artist's
>   friend Weir]
> Weir, Julian Alden, *The Grey Trellis,* 126, **126**
>   *See also* Hassam, Childe

La Farge, John, *Christ and the Disciples at Emmaus* (after Rembrandt), ***239***
Rembrandt Harmensz van Rijn, work after. *See* La Farge, John

Nast, Thomas, three illustrations for Poe's "The Raven," ***241, 242***
Poe, Edgar Allan, "The Raven" (Nast illustrations for), ***241, 242***

Indexing Art Works That Have "Missing" Information

In art books there is often the challenge of indexing captions that exhibit unavailable or missing information, such as unknown artists or untitled works. And sometimes there are images without page numbers.

Unknown Artists

When artist names are unknown, the works could be individually indexed by their titles. Or, they could be grouped together under "Unidentified ..." so that these entries would have the same structure as do the works listed under known artist names:

Unidentified artists, works by:
Lucia M. O. Streeter, c.1825 [a portrait]
Still Life: Fruit, c. 1840s
Yorktown and York River—As Seen from Top of a Tree at Camp Winfield Scott, 1862

Indexing Untitled Works of Art

The indexing of 20th-century or contemporary artworks that are captioned as "Untitled" can be complex. If there are a number of untitled works, then the indexer has to decide on a strategy for including them all while avoiding duplication by providing just enough "extra" information in the index headings to differentiate among similar titles. Any such strategy may be discussed with the client (editor or author) to reach agreement on the level of detail to include.

The next groups of entries show ways to index untitled objects that are all by the same artist. Adding such data as their different dates or dimensions could differentiate similar entries. Another strategy is to divide the objects into logical groups while still keeping the index entries reasonably short, avoiding long strings of page numbers whenever possible.[16]

For example, in the first group of entries below, the untitled artworks had a series identification as each main heading. Subheadings were differentiated first by year numbers (in chronological order) and then by photographic media names (in alphabetic order). Page numbers in *italics* were used for illustrations. Note that a plural subheading, such as "1976 color slides"—unlike "1974 color slide"—was used only because the 1976 subheading had page numbers referencing *more than one artwork* (or a series).

Untitled (Iowa series), 195

:

:

Untitled (Mexico series), 233
    1970s color photographs, 70, *142*, 143, 170, *170*, 172
    1974 color slide, *142*, 143
    1976 color slides, *34*, 35, 45, *45*, *158*, 159, *161*, *204*, 205
    1977 color slides, 170, *171*, 188, *188*
    1977 lifetime color photographs, 186, *186*, 188, *188*, 301
    1978 lifetime black & white photographs, 86, *86*, 126, *127*, 249, *249*,
       278, *278*
    1978 lifetime color photographs, *14*, 15, 32, *33*, 300
    1979 lifetime color photographs, 13, *13*, 68, *68*, 173, *173*, 178, *179*
    1980 color slide, *22*, 23
    1980 lifetime black & white photograph, 86, *87*

In the next group, there were originally 21 index headings representing 37 untitled works created between 1972 and 1985 by the same artist, however not all of them are shown below. The most manageable differentiations among these main headings for works with identical titles were chronological: by year, approximate year ("c1983"), or a span of years ("c1973–1980").

Untitled (1972), 40, *40*
Untitled (1973), 157, *157*, 160, *160*, 231
Untitled (c1973-1980), 26, *26*
Untitled (1974), 220, *220*
Untitled (1976), 160, *161*, 257n81

:

:

Untitled (1983), 104, *105*, 109, *109*
Untitled (c1983), 181, *181*
Untitled (c1983-84), 65, *65*, 124, *124*
Untitled (1984), 25, *25*, 99, 110, *110*, 114, *114*, *115*
Untitled (1985), 32, *32*, 119, *119*, 258n111
Untitled (c1985), 99, *99*, 240, *240*, 244, *244*, 247, *247*, 256, *256*, 260, *260*

Indexing Unnumbered Illustration Pages

The locations of illustrations are usually indicated by providing typographical differentiation for their page numbers, such as putting them in italics, boldface, or within square brackets. As noted earlier, the meanings of these number variations should be given in an introduction to the index. As Rowland and Brenner indicate (p. 31), often an art book index is expected to tell the reader whether a page includes both an image depicting the topic, *and* text information on a topic. In that case, a page number may be cited twice, once with the number in italics. If the caption is on a different page from that of the image, the caption page number may be cited as text. The following example is from Wendy Slatkin's "Appreciation" of painter Vigée-Lebrun,[17] the court portraitist for the queen of France:

> Vigée-Lebrun, Elisabeth, 328–330
>   *Marie Antoinette and Her Children,* 328–329, *329,* 330
>   *Portrait of Hubert Robert,* 329–330, *330*

When art book illustrations such as tipped in color plates have no page numbers, the entries may need special *identification numbers* instead (such as [**Plate 58**]), or *locator words.* Examples of the latter (sometimes given in italics or within parentheses) are *front cover, frontispiece, (plate facing 39),* or, for an unnumbered group of images: *photos in section after 62.* The placement order for locator words varies. Sometimes they are given in alphabetic order *after* all the regular text page numbers:

> 48–53, *74–75,* 109, *(back cover), (frontispiece), (plates in section after 75)*

and sometimes they are inserted in order of occurrence in the book:

> *front cover,* 39, *41,* 110, 374–375, *back inside cover*

Words for Images

The indexer does not illustrate the art book index with images, but instead makes a creative selection among the names and other topics, which appear in the text. The indexer may also include related terms *not* seen in the text. These are terms that have been discussed previously or are implied, or words for which the readers might search. The indexer may use *cross-references* to send the reader from synonyms or "outside terms" to the headings for terms and important concepts used in the book, or *double post* the synonyms, providing the same page numbers for each.

Equality of Headings

Index headings *look* equal. The terms are presented in the same format regardless of whether they refer to a single art object, a specific definition, or a broad concept discussed in the book. The text can be indexed by its "aboutness" (Svenonius's 1994 term, quoted in Wellisch, p. 332), that is, the ideas and topics discussed, explained, or refuted. The indexer looks both for in-depth discussions and substantive mentions to be indexed. The indexer may gather some index terms into related groups under main headings that reflect the most important themes in the text, and subdivide them into a number of subheading topics.

Image Content

The works of art reproduced in the art book may be examples of specific *genres* (visual works by subject type). For example, paintings may be presented in groups such as landscapes, portraits, still life *Vanitas* images, or history paintings. If the themes, meanings, and emotional impact of artworks are discussed, the indexer should concentrate on using the *author's words* for these abstract concepts whenever possible.

The indexer does not usually use her own words for *unmentioned visual content* observed within certain images, even if she knows, for instance, that Grant Wood's dentist modeled for the farmer in his painting "American Gothic." However, if a visual theme has been noted previously in the book, and it is visible again in later images without further text comment, these additional image page numbers may be added to the initial entry for that theme. The following examples are from the index to an illustrated material culture history book about traditional American vaquero bit and spur makers[18] [with some annotations added for this discussion]:

> buildings and shops:
> > interior views, 76, *177, 192, 195, 241, 243, 282*
> > saddlery business, *166, 169, 171, 182, 189, 231, 286, 295*
> design motifs, frequently used: [on spurs]
> > flowers, *92, 111, 116, 121, 153, 203*
> > "gal-leg," *74, 168*
> > Indians, *112, 114, 156*
> > Moorish, *138, 160, 195, 202, 204, 231, 273*
> Indians: [this authors' term reflects usage in the hand-crafted spurs era]
> > bit and spur makers, 123, 115
> > design motifs featuring, *112, 114, 156*
> > design motifs used by, *38, 57, 60, 71*

CONCLUSION

An artwork or material culture object without background information is almost like an undocumented "orphan." Information can enhance both the historic and monetary value of a collected object and even influence its preservation. It is notable that the experts on the *Antiques Roadshow* television programs seem to appreciate an object more, and even estimate a higher value, when the owner presents documents and photographs about the piece being examined.

In the 1970s and '80s I was active in the movement for increasing the recognition of contemporary and historic women artists and art professionals, a group struggle that continues today. I urged artists to keep the owners of their artworks informed by providing them not only with object creation information, but also with periodic exhibition news releases and artist résumé updates.[19] Further, it is often the case that contemporary or young artists' works may get documented only by printed ephemera, while not yet referenced or discussed in art books. I recommended that artists or galleries include in their art exhibition flyers and postcards information helpful to future researchers, such as full year numbers in exhibition dates, art image captions, and complete contact addresses. Curators and authors of art books may collect and study these materials to document the careers of men and women artists and their art objects.

The indexer of art books is part of a team that contributes to the "going down in history" of published works of art. We help future audiences find specific objects and discussions of concepts about them. And while writing an index, the indexer not only has the pleasure of seeing the images in beautifully designed books, but also the benefit of becoming further educated about art.

The art objects and their "careers" will continue long after we indexers complete our projects. In the indexes we write for art books and catalogs, the clear and accurate referencing of artworks, and of the ideas which inform them, is a legacy we can be proud of.

NOTE AND ACKNOWLEDGMENTS

All of the Endnotes reference art or art history publications indexed by the chapter author, Susan Coerr. In the index entry examples, the art book convention of using italic or bold page numbers indicates pages where artworks are illustrated. Books cited in the text are listed in References. Online site addresses are given in the text and some of them are described in References. Thanks are due to the helpful readers who offered good suggestions for this article: Nancy Humphreys (indexer), Lois Shumaker (librarian), and friends Janet Bell and Lynn Strandberg.

ENDNOTES

1. Belting, Hans, *The Image and Its Public in the Middle Ages, Form and Function of Early Paintings of the Passion.* New Rochelle, NY: Aristide D. Caratzas, 1989.
2. Mathews, Thomas F., *Armenian Gospel Iconography: Tradition of the Glajor Gospel, (Dumbarton Oaks Studies).* Washington, DC: Dumbarton Oaks Pub Service, 1991.
3. Trenton, Patricia, Ed., *Independent Spirits: Women Painters of the American West, 1890–1945.* Los Angeles: Autry Museum of Western Heritage, in association with the University of California Press, Los Angeles, CA, 1995.
4. Alexander, Leora, *Taste and Power: Furnishing Modern France.* Berkeley and Los Angeles: University of California Press, 1996.
5. Woodson and Kawakami, *Classical Kimono: Four Centuries of Fashion.* San Francisco: Asian Art Museum, 1997.
6. Berger, Patricia, *Empire of Emptiness: Buddhist Art and Political Authority in Qing China.* Honolulu: University of Hawaii Press, 2003.
7. Gilman, Carolyn, *Lewis & Clark: Across the Divide, The National Bicentennial Exhibition.* St. Louis: Missouri Historical Society, 2004.

8. Bennett, Anna Gray, *Five Centuries of Tapestry*, [collection catalog]. San Francisco: the Fine Arts Museums of San Francisco, 1992.

9. *Celebrating Modern Art: The Anderson Collection,* San Francisco Museum of Modern Art [Oct. 7, 2000–Jan. 15, 2001, exhibition catalog].

10. Organization of Women Architects, San Francisco: *OWA Newsletters Cumulative Index, 1972–1988.*

11. Lynn, Martha Drexler, *American Studio Glass: 1960-1990.* New York and Manchester: Hudson Hills Press, Neuberger Museum of Art, Purchase, New York, 2004, pp. 82, 84–85.

12. Thompson, E. N., *Defender of the Gate: The Presidio of San Francisco, A History from 1846–1995,* Historic Resource Study, Vol. I & II, Golden Gate National Recreation Area, California, National Park Service, 1997. (The five indexes are at the end of Volume II.)

13. Jashemski, Wilhelmina F., *The Gardens of Pompeii, Catalogue, Vol. II.* New Rochelle, NY: Caratzas Brothers, 1990.

14. Barriault, Anne B., *Spalliera Paintings of Renaissance Tuscany.* University Park, PA: Pennsylvania State University Press, 1994.

15. Entries for "Goodridge, Sarah" through "Unidentified Artists" (except Oppenheim) are modeled on some the author wrote for MacAdam, Barbara J., *Marks of Distinction: Two Hundred Years of American Drawings and Watercolors from the Hood Museum of Art,* New York and Manchester: Hudson Hills Press, 2005.

16. These examples are modeled on the author's index headings for the exhibition catalog *Ana Mendieta, Earth Body: Sculpture and Performance 1972–1985,* Olga M. Viso, Ed., Hirshhorn Museum and Sculpture Garden, Smithsonian Institution, Washington, DC and Hatje Cantz Publishers, 2004.

17. Slatkin, Wendy, quoted by Robert Bersson in *Worlds of Art,* Mountain View, CA: Mayfield Publishing, 1991, pp. 328–330.

18. Martin, Ned and Jody, *Bit and Spur Makers in the Vaquero Tradition: A Historical Perspective.* Nicasio, CA: Hawkhill Press, 1997.

19. "Finding Women," a conference panel reported [by Coerr] in the *WCA Newsletter* of the Women's Caucus for Art, Vol. X, No. 4, 1981, pp. 6–7, 10–11.

REFERENCES

BULLETIN of the American Society for Information Science and Technology (ASIS&T, www.asis.org*),* Vol. 30, No. 5, June/July 2004, "Museum Informatics" Special Section, Layna White, Guest Editor, pp. 9–26.

Kimball, Ward. *Art Masterpieces.* Los Angeles: Price/Stern/Sloan Publishers, Inc., 1964; 1975. (Unpaginated and, therefore, unindexed.)

Nicholas, Lynn H. *The Rape of Europa: The Fate of Europe's Treasures In the Third Reich and the Second World War.* New York: Alfred A. Knopf, Inc., 1994.

Rowland, Marilyn, and Diane Brenner. Indexing Art and Art History Materials. In *Indexing Specialties: History.* Medford, NJ: American Society of Indexers, published by Information Today, Inc., 1998 (pp. 27–34). Includes an "Appendix: Thesauri as Information Sources," by Diane Brenner and Alison Chipman (pp. 35–36), and an annotated Resources list (pp. 37–39).

Weinberg, Bella Haas. "Reviews of Art & Architecture Thesaurus, 2nd edition. Toni Petersen, Director, and Guide to Indexing and Cataloging with the Art & Architecture Thesaurus, edited by Toni Petersen and Patricia J. Barnett," (first published in 1995); reprinted in *Can You Recommend a Good Book on Indexing?.* Medford, NJ: American Society of Indexers, published by Information Today, Inc., 1998, pp. 95–103.

Wellisch, Hans H. *Indexing from A to Z* (2nd edition). New York: H. W. Wilson, 1995. ("Illustrations," pp. 196–199, and "Nonprint Materials," pp. 332–337; 342.)

ONLINE RESOURCES

See also sites mentioned in the chapter text:

The Achenbach Foundation for Graphic Arts (and the Prints and Drawings Department of the Fine Arts Museums of San Francisco) site has listings for types of prints and Common Print Terms under "What Is An Original Print?" *See* http://www.achenbach.org/0%7Eindex.html

The Getty Research Institute databases include these three at their site: http://www.getty.edu/research/conducting_research/vocabularies/aat

> AAT: "The Art & Architecture Thesaurus is a structured vocabulary of more than 133,000 terms, descriptions, bibliographic citations, and other information relating to fine art, architecture, decorative arts, archival materials, and material culture."

> TGN: "The Getty Thesaurus of Geographic Names is a structured, world-coverage vocabulary of 1.3 million names, including vernacular and historical names, coordinates, and place types, and descriptive notes, focusing on places important for the study of art and architecture."

> ULAN: "The Getty Union List of Artist Names is a structured vocabulary containing more than 225,000 names and biographical and bibliographic information about artists and architects, including a wealth of variant names, pseudonyms, and language variants."

Examples of information on sites where art is being collected or created only on the Internet are:

Mirapaul, Matthew. "Art Unfolds in a Search for Keywords," Today's Headlines, *The New York Times,* June 17, 2004. (http://www.nytimes.com/pages/todaysheadlines)

Mulvany, Nancy. *i-TORQUE* 18 (http://www.i-torque.us) (September 2004), "Links" column, 11, note on the Museum of Online Museums: http://coudal.com/moom.php.

Chapter 6

Real-World Considerations When Indexing Plant Names: Dealing with Text Problems and Index Restrictions

Thérèse Shere[1] with Lina B. Burton © 2005

Regardless of who the author or publisher may be, virtually every book that includes plant names, either common or scientific, also contains at least a few textual problems and quirks. Some of the most common of these problems are inconsistent use of plant names (for example, using the common name daylily in one place but the name *Hemerocallis* in another), using more than one common name for the same plant (such as using Virginia bluebells in one place and cowslip in another), and using scientific names (such as *Coreopsis*) as both common and scientific names in the same text. An indexer must consider the varying needs of different index users in handling these problems. More knowledgeable readers are more likely to be familiar with botanical names and to be interested in discussions of species and cultivars. Less expert readers are probably more likely to be familiar primarily with common names and to be interested in genus-level discussions.

At the same time, indexers of gardening, botanical, or horticultural material also have to cope with the ever-present problem of space restrictions. Rare indeed is the book where we have an ample number of lines with which to work. More often, we find ourselves hunting for some way to cut just 10—or 100 or more—lines! And, of course, we also must work within publishers' house styles, which sometimes may be rather unusual.

Occasionally we all need some guidance in dealing with these problems. The *Chicago Manual of Style, 15th edition*, provides general style guidelines for names of plants in sections 8.127–8.138, but many tricky situations faced by indexers are not addressed. The guidelines I present here are based on my own indexing experience, comparisons of many horticultural book indexes, and conversations with other

85

indexers in the specialty. They also incorporate my reader's perspective as a frequent *user* of books on plant-related subjects.

TEXT PROBLEMS AND QUIRKS

Inconsistent Use of Plant Names

This problem appears in virtually every garden book on the face of the earth! Why? There could be several reasons. Possibly several people wrote the book, leading to inconsistency in the text. Perhaps the editor was not as alert as he should have been, is new and still learning to work with horticultural material, or does not specialize in horticultural material and thus isn't aware of the importance of consistency in addressing plant names. Or maybe the author simply *liked* using all those different names. Whatever the case, we have to deal with these inconsistencies in our indexes. Following are some common situations and some suggested guidelines for resolving them.

1. *The common name appears on some pages without the botanical name accompanying it, and/or the botanical name appears on some pages without the common name.* In this case, all references to both names must be gathered at each entry. However, readers familiar with just one of the names will not find all of the information available when they turn to a page mentioning only the name they know, unless each name appears parenthetically in the index after its mate, thus providing the alternative name for which they should look in the text.

Example: Adobe lily appears on pp. 26, 39, 144, 148
            Fritillaria pluriflora appears on pp. 144 and 152

Possible index entries:

Best: Here, all references have been gathered together. No matter which name the reader is familiar with, she will find all references to the plant and recognize those references on the page. (In this case, the index also serves as a learning tool —if the reader looks up adobe lily often enough, eventually she will remember *Fritillaria.*)

Adobe lily *(Fritillaria pluriflora),* 26, 39, 144, 148, 152
Fritillaria pluriflora (adobe lily), 26, 39, 144, 148, 152

Unacceptable: The following example is unacceptable because all references to the plant are not gathered together. The reader who knows only the common name will find different pages from those found by the reader who looks up the botanical name.

> Adobe lily, 26, 39, 144, 148
> *Fritillaria pluriflora,* 144, 152

The next example is also unacceptable. Here, the page numbers are gathered together in each of the two entries, but the reader who knows only the common name won't know, when he reads page 152, that *Fritillaria pluriflora* is the plant being sought. A reader who knows the botanical name but not the common name will be confused when she doesn't find *Fritillaria* on pp. 26, 39, and 148.

> Adobe lily, 26, 39, 144, 148, 152
> *Fritillaria pluriflora,* 26, 39, 144, 148, 152

Compromise: Here, all references have been gathered together. It doesn't matter if the reader is unfamiliar with one of the two names. Although it does add an extra step for the reader who looks up the common name, it's an excellent space-saving device for the indexer, because it often saves a line from wrapping.

> Adobe lily. See *Fritillaria pluriflora*
> *Fritillaria pluriflora* (adobe lily), 26, 39, 144, 148, 152

2. *The same situation as above can occur with an added complication: more than one common name.* In this case, two or more common names appear on various pages without the botanical name accompanying them, and/or the botanical name appears on some pages unaccompanied by the common names.

Example: Checkerbloom appears on pp. 26, 39, and 157
Wild hollyhock appears on pp. 28, 157, 263, and 264
Sidalcea appears on pp. 157–59

Possible index entries:

Best: As above, all references to the plant have been gathered together at each version of the name. It doesn't matter if the reader knows only one of the names —she will find everything available in the text about the plant and be able to recognize the unfamiliar name on the text page.

> Checkerbloom (wild hollyhock) *(Sidalcea),* 26, 28, 39, 157–59, 263, 264
> *Sidalcea* (checkerbloom, wild hollyhock), 26, 28, 39, 157–59, 263, 264
> Wild hollyhock (checkerbloom) *(Sidalcea),* 26, 28, 39, 157–59, 263, 264

Unacceptable: As with the first unacceptable solution in situation 1, all references have not been gathered together. The reader will not find the entries for
the names with which she is unfamiliar.

> Checkerbloom, 26, 39, 157
> Wild hollyhock, 28, 157, 263, 264
> *Sidalcea,* 157–59

As with the second unacceptable example in situation 1, in the following example all references have been gathered together but there is no clue given to the
reader as to which alternate name he is looking for when the referenced page is
reached.

> Checkerbloom, 26, 28, 39, 157–59, 263, 264
> Wild hollyhock, 26, 28, 39, 157–59, 263, 264
> *Sidalcea,* 26, 28, 39, 157–59, 263, 264

Compromise: Again, the compromise gathers all references together in one
place, using cross-references from the common names to the scientific name.
Although it does add a step for readers looking up either of the common names,
it is an excellent way to reduce the number of line wraps in the index without
compromising its integrity.

> Checkerbloom. *See Sidalcea*
> *Sidalcea* (checkerbloom, wild hollyhock), 26, 28, 39, 157–59,
>   263, 264
> Wild hollyhock. *See Sidalcea*

*3.   Text uses common name and botanical name in different places, but
never equates the two.* You think they are the same plant, but the text does not
actually say so. There are other plants besides *Colocasia esculenta* that you
have seen referred to as "elephant's ear," so there's a chance they really are
different.

Example: *Colocasia esculenta* appears on p. 119
              Elephant's ear appears on p. 202

In this situation, you should query the editor/author: "Are these the same
plant?" If the answer is "yes," your problem is solved. Even if the text is not
changed to clarify the issue for the reader, you can do so by adding the other
name parenthetically in the index and putting all the page references in each
entry:

Index entries: *Colocasia esculenta* (elephant's ear), 119, 202
                 Elephant's ear *(Colocasia esculenta)*, 119, 202

If it's not possible to query, or if the answer is unknown, there is little to be done. You'll have to simply index as the names appear in the text, without equating the two names:

Index entries: *Colocasia esculenta,* 202
                 Elephant's ear, 119

Just remind yourself "I did not write this book...I did not edit this book! I did not write this book...I did not edit this book!" You should make a note about your suspicion that the two plants are the same and include it with the index, in your list of errors found while working on the text, and hope that both text and index can be clarified somewhere down the line.

4. Same common name used for more than one plant. Sometimes the text makes it clear that the same common name is being used for more than one plant species, but if it doesn't, you should query the editor. The index entries for the common names will need to include the botanical name as a qualifier, even if you are not doing this for other common names in the index.

Index entries: Dusty miller *(Artemisia stellerana),* 166
                 Dusty miller *(Chrysanthemum ptarmiciflorum),* 228
                 Dusty miller *(Senecio cineraria),* 482

If absolutely essential, you could omit the species names, substituting "sp." or "spp." if appropriate:

                 Dusty miller *(Artemisia sp.),* 166
          or   Dusty miller *(Artemisia),* 166

Compound Common Names

Many common names are compounds of one or more modifiers and a noun. Examples include Norway maple, sweet gum, Douglas fir, sword fern, coast live oak, Mexican tulip poppy. Compound common names like these are inherently difficult to deal with.

The publisher may have its own preferred method of handling this issue. If not, you must decide whether to post such names in natural-language order (i.e., Norway maple), sorting alphabetically in the index on the modifier (in this case Norway); inverting and sorting on the noun element of the name (in this case Maple); or to do both by double-posting. Ideally, you would double-post, but space restrictions or house style may prevent this. If you must choose one or the other, let me emphasize that there is nothing scientific about these indexing decisions. They have to be made on a case-by-case basis. The following general guidelines will be useful.

Example: Norway maple, 59, 202   (natural order)
            Maple, Norway, 59, 202   (inverted)

According to Hans Wellisch, natural order is usually desirable because people who speak English tend to search for compound phrases on the modifying adjective, not the noun that follows it. As he so succinctly puts it, *"inverted headings should be avoided altogether in indexing."*[2] (emphasis in original). However, there are times, when inversion is desirable and, in fact, is the clearest way in which to present plant names and relationships.

1. Inverted index entries are desirable in the following situations:

a) *When the compound name is one of several discussed that share the same noun element.* Often this will be the common name for a genus. (In the following example, botanical names have been omitted for simplicity, but if space permits, include them, as mentioned above.)

Example: Coast live oak
            Cork oak
            Engelmann oak
            Oak
                    coast live
                    cork
                    Engelmann
                    pin
                    red
            Pin oak
            Red oak

If space considerations prohibit double-posting, inversion is generally preferable to natural order. This is a common style for field guides. In this example, you could save five lines by using only the inverted form:

Example: Oak
                    coast live
                    cork
                    Engelmann
                    pin
                    red

b) *When the compound name is one of several sharing the same noun element (genus), as above, and the text has genus-level information (i.e., culture, diseases, pests) that you do not want readers to miss.*

Example: Coast live oak. *See* Oak, coast live
Cork oak. *See* Oak, cork
Engelmann oak. *See* Oak, Engelmann
Oak
      coast live
      cork
      cultural problems
      diseases
      Engelmann
      pests
      pin
      red
Pin oak. *See* Oak, pin
Red oak. *See* Oak, red

In this case, if you put locators at the natural-order entries, readers would miss the generic information on cultural problems, pests, and diseases of oaks. It is rare that sufficient line space exists in indexes for double-posting all of the cultural information under each of the natural-language entries. Therefore, the inverted form is the better choice. An alternative would be to list the pages at the natural-language order entries and add a cross-reference, space permitting:

Coast live oak, 118, 253
    See also Oak

c) *When there is a possibility of confusion.*

Example: Foxglove *(Digitalis)*
Foxglove, wild *(Penstemon cobaea)*
Wild foxglove *(Penstemon cobaea)*

Douglas fir *(Pseudotsuga menziesii)*
Fir *(Abies)*
Fir, Douglas *(Pseudotsuga menziesii)*

In cases like these, if space precludes double-posting, I would stick with the natural order; the inversion is "extra help" for readers but it's probably not the first place they'll look.

2. Natural-order index entries are desirable in these situations:

a) *When the noun element is a common name for a genus, and the compound common name is for a totally unrelated plant that wouldn't be confused with the genus.*

Example: Laurel *(Laurus nobilis)*
                       Mountain laurel *(Kalmia latifolia)*

NOT   Laurel, mountain *(Kalmia latifolia)*

b) *When the noun element is very generic.*

Example: Buffalo grass   NOT Grass, buffalo
                       Butterfly bush   NOT Bush, butterfly

However, there may be circumstances where you want to call attention to, for example, grasses as a group, distinct from the other plants in the book. Such might be the case when you can mentally "hear" the reader saying, "Well, I know it's some kind of ornamental grass, but I haven't the slightest idea which one." (This kind of situation is most likely to occur with plants that many people are relatively unfamiliar with, such as the grasses, ferns, cacti, and mosses.) By grouping them together, you narrow the reader's choices. Even if she does not know the name of the plant, it is possible to run down the list until one is found that matches the plant being sought. Such a list might look like this:

> Ornamental grasses. *See also* Lawn grasses; Weedy grasses
>   big bluestem *(Andropogon)*, 181
>   black dragon *(Ophiopogon)*, 908
>   blue fescue *(Festuca)*, 137–38, 181
>   mesquite grass *(Bouteloua)*, 721

In this case, sorting was done on the common name, with the genus name only in parentheses to save space. The name used for sorting could just as easily have been the botanical name, with the common name in parentheses.

c) *When the inverted form just doesn't make sense.*

Example: Miller, dusty
                       Breath, baby's
                       Lace, Queen Anne's

(You can have lots of fun thinking up more of these!)

Botanical Names Used as Common Names

Some plants are commonly known by their scientific genus names: chrysanthemum, magnolia, zinnia, daphne, for example. Garden books often present such names in roman type and lowercased. Many garden books go so far as to use these names both in roman type, lowercased *and* in italic type, with the genus name initially capped, sometimes within the same paragraph. In these cases, sometimes you can just omit the common name typography from the entry and use the botanical name only.

Example: *Daphne,* 64, 89

Or, if adding the common name won't cause a wraparound line, eating up space, you could also index this as follows:

Example: Daphne (*Daphne*), 64, 89

This is the way one well-known publisher prefers to handle this type of situation; it makes it absolutely clear to the reader that the common name and the scientific name are the same.

Often, however, we encounter more complexity. For instance, the genus name may be used as a common name, but in fact refers to just a single member of the genus:

Example: Calliopsis *(Coreopsis tinctoria),* 89
                   Coreopsis
                       lanceolata (coreopsis), 119, 178
                       tinctoria (calliopsis), 89
                 Coreopsis *(Coreopsis lanceolata),* 119, 178

Or, a genus name may be used as a common name for members of two genera:

Example: *Keckiella*
                   cordifolius, 109
                   corymbosus, 109
               Penstemon
                   azureus, 113, 115, 260, 265
                   speciosus, 37, 116, 265, 266
               Penstemon
                   azure *(Penstemon azureus),* 113, 115, 260, 265
                   climbing *(Keckiella cordifolius),* 109
                   red foothill *(K. corymbosus),* 109
                   showy *(P. speciosus),* 37, 116, 265, 266

These situations may require forcing the sort order of the entries, so that the *Penstemon* and penstemon entries, for example, do not interfile, causing utter confusion for the poor reader.

When common names and genus names are close, but not identical, both forms should be given, but you should omit either the common name entry or the botanical name entry, since they will sort right next to each other:

> Lily *(Lilium)*   or   *Lilium* (lily)
> Rose *(Rosa)*   *Rosa* (rose)
> Tulip *(Tulipa)*   *Tulipa* (tulip)

You could provide a cross-reference as well:

> *Lilium. See* lily
> Lily *(Lilium)*

Genus-Level vs. Species-Level Discussions Using Common Names

Indexers must be careful to understand and sort out discussions of genera from discussions of species. This process can lead to complex common-name entries like this one, which mixes subentries for an unaccompanied common name, two different genera, and a species:

Example: Elm, 156, 160, 170, 182, 187, 236
> American *(Ulmus)*, 158, 221
> Asian *(Zelkova)*, 168, 191
> European *(Ulmus)*, 93, 168, 221
> Siberian *(U. pumila)*, 93, 219

Since you have no idea which of the elms are being referenced on pages 156, 160, 170, 182, 187, and 236, you have no choice but to either query the editor for clarification or, if this doesn't work, to list these locators as shown here.

You also want to be sure that readers who look up a common name for a species will not miss genus-level information, as discussed above.

A-Z Text Formats

Garden books often use an A–Z encyclopedia-style format for part, but not all, of the text, with the encyclopedia usually being organized by botanical name. This can pose several problems for indexers.

1. The editors may ask that the A–Z section not be indexed. Often it is necessary to index one or two introductory chapters, but not the main A–Z part of the book.

This can be fine, *if* the A–Z text contains entries for common names that are cross-referenced to botanical names. Here's an example of an easy-to-understand format:

Example: Poppy. See *Papaver*
             Poppy, Himalayan. See *Meconopsis betonicifolia*
             Poppy mallow. See *Callirhoe involucrata*
             Populus [followed by a lengthy discussion on this genus,
                 along with several of its species]
             Porcupine grass. See *Miscanthus sinensis* 'Strictus'

If common names are not included in the encyclopedia listing with cross-references to the botanical names, readers unfamiliar with the botanical names would have no way to find them and the usefulness of the book would be severely impaired.

If an encyclopedia section is not indexed, another problem arises: When there is information about specific plants in the nonencyclopedic section of the book as well as in the encyclopedia proper. In this case you might have numerous index entries for specific plants with page references for those introductory chapters, but no page listing for the plant's primary entry in the encyclopedia—not an ideal situation.

Example: Crabapple *(Malus)* appears in plant lists or introductory material
             on pp. 22, 54, and 56; the main discussion of the plant is in the
             A-Z section on page 289.

Index entries: Crabapple *(Malus),* 22, 54, 56
                Malus (crabapple), 22, 54, 56

It's very important in this case to include a head note at the beginning of the index, which tells the reader that the listings in the encyclopedia section are not indexed.

Example: This index covers pages 1 to 376. You will find some entries for
             specific plants in the index; however, additional information for
             individual plants appears in the Encyclopedia of Plants, which
             begins on page 377.

2. Indexing the encyclopedia listings. When you *do* index an encyclopedia section, often all or almost all references to a particular genus will occur on one page. If there is discussion of several different species and you include each as a subentry, this can lead to redundant-looking entries.

Example: *Angelica,* 178
                    breweri, 178
                    hendersonii, 178
                    lineariloba, 178
                    tomentosa, 178

In this situation it's usually best to drop the subentries and make an entry for the genus only:

              Angelica species, 178
or   *Angelica* spp., 178
or   *Angelica,* 178

The first two examples are better than the last, because they give the reader a clue that more than one species is discussed on that page.

Frequently there will be just one or two mentions of a particular species on other pages as well.

Example: Encyclopedia entry for genus *Erysimum* appears on p. 171; five
              species are discussed there. One of those species also appears in
              a plant list on p. 29; another is illustrated on p. 170.

Possible index entries:
              Erysimum (wallflower), 171
                    capitatum, 171
                    concinnum, 171
                    franciscanum, 29, 171
                    grandiflorum, 170, 171
                    menziesii, 171
              Wallflower *(Erysimum),* 29, *170,* 171

or   *Erysimum* spp. (wallflower), 29, *170,* 171
              Wallflower *(Erysimum),* 29, *170,* 171

In these instances, the choice between these two entry methods depends on two factors: the book's audience and space requirements. Knowledgeable readers are probably more likely to be looking for species-level information in the index and would prefer to see species listed, if possible. You could leave out the abbreviation "spp.," but to do so is inadvisable since it does provide the reader with a useful clue that several species are contained in the page references.

Expert Tip

Consider the audience if you have to make a choice between the common and the scientific name—cross-reference from one to the other.

Note that in the *Erysimum* examples, a difference of five lines exists between the two examples. A savings of five lines per double-posted entry throughout the index could result in an index that is much too short for the space allowed, leaving blank pages at the end. Some publishers don't consider this a problem. For others, however, it is a hanging offense! So you need to keep in mind the number of lines you have to work with and adjust accordingly.

Unacceptable: Including only two of the species and omitting the other three species from the subentry list. This gives the erroneous impression that the two that *are* listed are the only ones discussed in the book.

Example: Erysimum (wallflower), 171
    franciscanum, 29, 171
    grandiflorum, 170, 171

Deleting the species names as subentries raises another issue. Suppose you have a common name entry for one of the species. If the common name bluff wallflower is given for *Erysimum concinnum,* you have two possible forms for the common name entry:

Bluff wallflower *(Erysimum concinnum),* 171
or Bluff wallflower. See *Erysimum concinnum*

If you do not list species as subentries under *Erysimum,* you cannot use the *See* reference because the reader won't find its target entry.

Text Organized by Plant Families

Sometimes long sections of a book will be organized by plant family, with genera listed alphabetically within the sections.

Example: Sunflower family genera are listed from p. 230 to p. 249. The only mention of the family *per se* is on p. 230.

Index entry: Sunflower family *(Asteraceae, Compositae),* 230
                See also specific genera

If there were no specific discussion of the family at all, just listings of genera, you could make the entry like this:

                Sunflower family *(Asteraceae, Compositae),* 230–49
                See also specific genera

or   Sunflower family *(Asteraceae, Compositae). See specific genera*

The first example, which lists a page range (230–49), is preferable. If you use only the *See* reference, readers who don't know which genera belong to the family will be lost. Note: Families, too, have both common and scientific names, just like genera and species. You may need to make entries for both.

Plant Lists

Often some of the most useful information in a book is contained in plant lists. Alas, sometimes indexers are directed not to index their contents. Well-edited books present all plant lists consistently in the same format, with both botanical name and common name, if present, given.

If your book has common-name-only plant lists, beware! You'll have to be certain of the plants' identities so you can add the page references to the botanical name entries. Also, if more than one common name is used for a plant, each may show up in a separate plant list; you'll need to make sure such references are gathered together, as discussed above.

Illustrations and Captions

Photographs and illustrations in garden books can be problematic for indexers. If you're lucky, you'll have well-written captions that list all the major plants in the photo, so they are easily indexed. Often captions will have common names only, so you'll have to be careful about botanical name identification. Sometimes a clearly identifiable plant is in the photo, but not mentioned in the caption. I think it's best to index such appearances, after checking with the editor. Often, though, the pages the indexer receives have poor copies of the photos, or the photos are missing entirely—in which case you've only the captions to go on.

In some garden books photos are bound in as an insert. Ideally, if the insert pages are not numbered, the photos will be identified by plate numbers that you can use as locators.

Example: *Salvia disjuncta,* 65–66, 195, 201, 207, 208, Plate 89

If not, you'll have to come up with another locator scheme. Fortunately, this doesn't happen often!

Books Devoted to a Single Genus

Books devoted to a single genus are common. In these specialized books, I prefer to list species names as main entries instead of subentries, because the text is focused at the species level and much of the information discussed is species-specific. If cultivars are discussed, they can be given as either subentries or as part of the species entry, repeating the genus and species names for each entry.

Example: *Salvia farinacea,* 74–76, 97, 115, 207
'Blue Bedder,' 75, 76,
'Mina,' 75, 199
'Victoria,' 75, 76, 94, 173, 199

or   *Salvia farinacea,* 74–76, 97, 115, 207
Salvia farinacea 'Blue Bedder,' 75, 76, 199
Salvia farinacea 'Mina,' 75, 199
Salvia farinacea 'Victoria,' 75, 76, 94, 173, 199

To my eye, the first choice "reads" more easily, and requires less line space, but both techniques are common and correct.

The *Salvia* examples above work well for a book devoted to that genus, but which also mentions lots of other plants used, for example, as companions to the *Salvias.*

In some books on a single plant, the variety or cultivar names alone may become the main entries. For example, a book on roses that discusses hundreds of cultivars, and no (or few) other genera would more appropriately be indexed by cultivar name, as is the case with the following example.

Example: Aloha
Alpine Sunset
Altissimo
Amanecer
Amaryllis josephinae
Amatsu-Otome
Amber Queen

Note that in this case, the companion plant, *Amaryllis josephinae,* is listed among the cultivars but stands out distinctly because it is italicized, as it should be.

If species are discussed as well as cultivars, however, the species must be listed under the full binomial:

Example: Rocky
                      Rödhätte
                      Roger Lamberlin
                      Romance
                      Romanze
                      Rosa alba
                      Rosa arkansana

Expert Tip

Note that in both of these cases, the indexer has chosen not to enclose the cultivar names in single quotation marks. Although technically incorrect, it does arguably make the list of entries more readable, and saves the indexer some keystrokes; however, this should not be done without the editor's permission.

Also while it is accepted practice (by most) to separate the genus and species names by placing genus name on one line and making the species name a subentry on a second line beneath it, you absolutely *cannot* make the species name (i.e., *alba, arkansana*) the main entry. Species names cannot stand alone. The proper main entries are *Rosa alba* and *Rosa arkansana*.

Texts Requiring Mixed Subentry Types in the Index

A common problem arises for indexers when species names as subentries (or sub-subentries) must be mixed with other subentries referring to subjects, rather than plant species. It can look awkward to have the two subentry types interfiled.

Example: *Acer* (maple), 45, 71, 120–121, 236, 237
                    diseases, 120–121, 208, 242, 256
                        palmatum (Japanese maple), 6, 236, 252
                        pests, 121, 147, 157, 167, 184, 195
                        platanoides (Norway maple), 207, 256
                        rubrum (red maple), 39, *44,* 45
                        saccharinum (silver maple), 45, 157, 256
                        saccharum 'Caddo' (Caddo maple), 51
                    wind-resistant selections, 236

The common name entry for Maple would look almost as awkward, although at least all the subentries would begin with roman type. When entries like this grow very, very long (say, a full column, in a book that devotes a great deal of discussion to one genus or species), this interfiling becomes quite objectionable, and begins to interfere with usability. You may want to group each of the two subentry types within the list by adding a sub-subentry level. Sometimes this can be done via clever wording, without breaking any indexing rules:

Example: Tomato, **119–138**
                   diseases, 120–122
                   early-maturing varieties, 124
                   pests, 122–123
                   planting and care, 119–120
                   varieties listed, 125–138
                           'Beefmaster,' 127
                           'Brandywine,' 127
                           'Early Girl,' 129
                           'Green Grape,' 130
                           'San Francisco Fog,' 136
                           'Sweet 100,' 137
                           (etc.)

Example: Rose *(Rosa)*, 20, 28, 76, **228–242**
                   care and planting, 228–229
                   choosing varieties, 232–233, 240
                   pictured, *16, 20–21, 49, 77*
                           'Abraham Darby,' 228
                           'Dortmund,' 231
                           'Fragrant Cloud,' 233
                           (etc.)
                   in plans
                           'China Doll,' 115
                           'French Lace,' 127
                           'New Dawn,' 127
                           (etc.)
                   species and cultivars listed, 235–242
                           'Angel Face,' 235
                           'Cécile Brunner,' 236
                           'Don Juan,' 236
                           'Golden Rambler,' 237
                           'Mr. Lincoln,' 238
                           'White Wings,' 242

(etc.)
R. banksiae, 240
R. chinensis, 240
R. gallica, 240
R. moyesii, 241
(etc.)

Notice how I have forced the sort in the example above so that 'White Wings' sorts before the italicized species entries. This is a pretty subtle example of breaking the rules to make the entry more readable. You might go all out, with the editor's permission, and really break the rules, listing subentries in the most readable fashion, even if that moves them far out of alphabetical order. If there are going to be many subentries, this can really help the reader in navigating. This example breaks sorting rules in order to group all the species together and all the cultivars together. All subentries for other information about the genus are grouped at the top of the entry:

Example: *Narcissus,* 23, 26, 198–205
                   allergies to, 59
                   classification of, 199–200, 202–5
                   flower form, 8
                   lifting and storing bulbs, 46
                   water requirements, 59
                   asturiensis, 203
                   canaliculatus, 204
                   (several more species names follow)
                   cultivars:
                         'Actaea,' 203
                         'Baby Moon,' 203
                         (many more cultivar names follow)

SPACE RESTRICTIONS

I find that space restrictions, often very severe, are an almost omnipresent problem. Here are some strategies for dealing with them, more or less in the order I would use them.

1. Suggest a single index instead of separate subject and plant name indexes. Although it is fairly rare for an editor to request separate subject and plant name indexes, if he has done so, suggest that you be allowed to combine the two. You'll save the space of the break between them (i.e., the space that the header for the second index will consume). These can be precious lines in a pinch.

2. *Streamline entries for plant names line by line to shorten them.*

a) *If it will actually save space, use the* See *reference to reduce the number of lines used.* If, however, the locators don't cause the line to wrap, leave them alone.

Example: Ivy *(Hedera)*, 224, 226

     but   Maple. See *Acer*   (where *Acer* has an entry taking 10 lines)

Sometimes you may want to direct readers from the botanical name entries to the common name entries, instead of the other way around. Such would be the case if the target audience is less knowledgeable about plants, if the text is organized by common name, or if the book's topic is broader than the plants themselves (such as a craft book). Put the locators where you think most readers will look first.

b) *Drop parenthetic common names following botanical names.* For a well-edited book in which the common and botanical names always appear together, this presents no problems. If the reader will be sent to pages that contain only the common name, it is not ideal, but you can argue that a reader knowledgeable enough to look up the botanical name is likely to recognize the common name when she sees it.

Example: *Sisyrinchium bellum* (blue-eyed grass)   (original version)

    cut to   *Sisyrinchium bellum*

c) *Drop species names from parenthetic botanical names where it will keep a line from wrapping.*

Example: Blue-eyed grass *(Sisyrinchium bellum)*   (original version)

    cut to   Blue-eyed grass *(Sisyrinchium)*

Although not technically correct, this would not pose a practical problem unless more than one species of *Sisyrinchium* appeared on one of the pages referenced without the common names, making it impossible for the reader to know which one was blue-eyed grass. I would drop the *entire* parenthetic botanical name only in cases of dire necessity, and only if the botanical name appeared with the common name in the text.

3. Shorten whole classes of entries. Sunset's *Western Garden Book* gives only the locator for the encyclopedia listing of a plant at the common name entry. Only the botanical name entries contain all the page references. This scheme obviously requires a head note, and I find it rather odd. However, unusual schemes like this can work fine for books that will be consulted over and over, because readers will learn the index's structure.

4. Delete entire entries. As discussed earlier, delete species names as subentries and double-posting of compound common names where possible.

5. Condense locators.

a) *Use special typography to cut the number of locators.* For instance, use bolding to indicate a page range for a main discussion that includes illustrations so you don't need separate locators for the illustrations. (Warning: This must be done consistently throughout the entire index, not just here and there, as needed, and a head note will be required to explain the typography.) Thus, if Rose (*Rosa*) is discussed on pages 111–119 and 235, with illustrations on pages 112, 113, 114, 115, and 236, you could truncate the entry as follows:

Example: Rose *(Rosa)*, **111–119**, 235, *236*

instead of   Rose *(Rosa)*, 111–119, *112, 113, 114, 115*, 235, *236*

A head note for this type of entry might read as follows: "Page references in **bold type** indicate encyclopedia entries, which always contain photographs. Page references in *italic type* indicate additional illustrations."

b) Condense strings of locators for separate mentions on consecutive pages into page ranges. Although it is preferable not to do this for separate text mentions, particularly if text on other plants exists between the mentions, I find it less objectionable if the material being dealt with in this manner consists of illustrations on consecutive pages. Thus:

Example: Ivy *(Hedera)*, *54–56*, 59

instead of   Ivy *(Hedera)*, *54, 55, 56*, 59

6. Delete whole classes of entries as a last resort. If you've begun by including them, you could omit botanical names of vegetables and fruits, for instance. For a book that discusses pests or weeds where the scientific name of each is given parenthetically just once, in the subject's main entry, you could omit those scientific name entries. It is highly unlikely that a general reader would look up vegetables, fruits, pests, or weeds under their scientific names; they generally don't know what those names are. When I indexed Sunset's *Western Garden Problem Solver,* space was so short that I ended up deleting *all* the botanical name entries, which made up about 10 percent of the index lines. I justified the decision for myself by noting that the plant-specific sections of the book were organized entirely by common name, and the book had a problem-solving focus, which meant there were many more non-plant entries than plant name entries. Half the plants mentioned were weeds, plants that index users would be most likely to look up by their common names.

7. *Use run-in format.* The run-in format for subentries is not as common as it used to be in gardening books, but you do still run across it. It can be a great space saver in some situations. In the following example, two lines have been saved by this format.

Example: *Aquilegia,* 28, 29, **91–92**; *eximia,* 32, **91**; *formosa,* 28,
32, **91**, 262, 264; *pubescens,* 37, 41, **92**

As a practical matter, the run-in format is suitable *only* when there is one subentry level. However, you could also use a hybrid format, with subentries indented, and sub-subentries in run-in style. The *Chicago Manual of Style* (15th edition) now recommends this hybrid style for all indexes that use sub-subentries. I find it works well for some types of books, but horticultural indexes can be difficult to read formatted in this way:

Example: Rose *(Rosa),* 20, 28, 76, **228–242**
care and planting, 228–229
choosing varieties, 232–233, 240
pictured, *16, 20–21, 49, 77;* 'Abraham Darby,' *228;*
'Dortmund,' *231;* 'Fragrant Cloud,' *233*
in plans: 'China Doll,' 115; 'French Lace,' 127; 'New Dawn,' 127
species and cultivars listed, 235–242; 'Angel Face,' 235;
'Cécile Brunner,' 236; 'Don Juan,' 236; 'Golden Rambler,' 237;
'Mr. Lincoln,' 238; 'White Wings,' 242; *R. banksiae,* 240; *R.*
chinensis, 240; R. gallica, 240; R. moyesii, 241

CLIENT-IMPOSED FORMAT/STYLE RESTRICTIONS

A client frequently will impose certain restrictions on index format and style, either for all of its books or on a book-by-book basis. I've found that if such a restriction will compromise the index, I can often make a case to the client and get it lifted. A simple explanation of why a practice is necessary, combined with an assurance that the index will fit in the available space, often suffices.

Other times, the in-house stylistic criteria are non-negotiable and may strike you as distinctly different, if not, in fact odd.

For example, one client separates the subject index from the plant name index. They also use roman type for all main-entry botanical names,

Example: Artemisia stelleriana

However, if the names are in parentheses, this client asks that the parenthetical name be italicized:

Example: Dusty miller (*Artemisia stelleriana*)

According to every authority that I've read on this question, botanical names should be italicized. Nevertheless, I don't believe the index is seriously compromised by setting the botanical names in roman type; in any case, this is the house style they've used for years and I doubt very seriously if they're about to change it now.

Other clients may prefer that plant lists not be indexed, or that the lists in a particular book not be indexed. In this situation, I might point out to the editor that the plant lists contain some of the most valuable information about the specific plants, and if it is not indexed, the information may be lost to the reader. Usually, indexing the lists means adding only a few locators to already-existing entries and can be handled within space limitations.

Other clients may not allow parenthetical common or scientific names in the index. This issue may be resolved by pointing out how much more useful an index containing such references is to the reader in finding all references to a particular plant. It also helps to have a good example available—perhaps from another book you've indexed—which you can fax to them so they'll see how it looks. This may be a visualization issue—they simply can't "see" it unless you show it to them.

Some garden book indexes use a *See* reference from every common name entry, sending readers to the botanical name, a practice that the reader may find annoying—she has to look two places instead of one to find the locator. In this case, the common name entries for species will require separate species subentries under the genus name, as discussed earlier. A head note warning the reader that locators are under the botanical name may be helpful in this instance.

Other clients may not allow subentries to repeat locators that appear in the main entry. This editing decision overlooks the many different kinds of distinct kinds of information that can appear on a single page. Omitting locator subentries makes it much harder for the reader to find detailed information or information on a specific subtopic. At the same time, omitting locator entries from the general heading prevents quick access to the general, lengthy discussion on the subject.

Sometimes client education is helpful. In this regard, the information presented here should give you some ammunition. For example, you might point out that it's common practice to have combined subject and plant-name indexes and combining them will save space so that you won't have to delete crucial entries. Once you understand the pros and cons of, for example, including both common and scientific names in each plant name entry, you can explain to your editor why this is a good idea and give examples, emphasizing the confusion that can be avoided when plants in different genera have the same common name. The editor may never have thought about the reasons for doing this before.

Sometimes house style requests are odd, but this is an issue that is generally not worth arguing about. My advice: Choose your battles and don't get heartburn over client criteria about which you disagree but that are non-negotiable! Remember, it may be your index, but it's *their* book.

ENDNOTES

1. Based on a paper presented by Thérèse Shere at ASI National Conference, Gardening/Environmental Studies SIG Seminar and Workshop, "Indexing Scientific and Common Names: Real World Considerations," May 12, 2000. Edited for publication by Lina B. Burton, Melinda D. Davis, Hannah Huse, Thérèse Shere, and Ann Truesdale.
2. Hans Wellisch. *Indexing from A to Z,* 2nd edition. (New York, Dublin: H. W. Wilson, 1995) p. 75.

Chapter 7

Indexing for the Computer Industry

Beth Palmer © 2005

When I was a software developer, my fellow engineers were always amused by my history. With advanced degrees in both English and Computer Science, I was an anomaly in the computer business.

It didn't take many years of working as a software developer before I realized that I didn't enjoy it. Fortunately for me, my company's two technical writers both left within weeks of each other. I offered to step in and spent much of the next year writing, editing, and (yes!) indexing all the company manuals.

Unfortunately, the company seemed to feel that paying an engineer's salary to a technical writer was inappropriate. So it was back to software development for me. But I'd learned a lot.

Several years later, I left my programming job to work as a full-time freelance indexer. Most of my work to date has been on technical subjects, and the 15 years I spent in the business have been undeniably helpful.

Whether or not you have a background similar to mine, you *can* index computer-related topics. I'll cover here some of the issues you need to consider and describe here some of the unique aspects of this work.

Do you have to be a computer guru to index computer subjects?

No, but it helps.

Just like any other type of indexing, specialized knowledge is useful. However, even if you don't have 15 years of experience in the computer industry, you can index these subjects if you're willing to learn the terminology.

If you don't have a background in the industry, I advise you—at least in the beginning—to stick with indexable material written for nontechies (like the *Dummies* series). In this genre you will be able to approach the material from the same perspective as the reader—the best way to index.

What makes the subject of computer technology different for indexers?

There are two answers: purpose and terminology.

THE PURPOSE OF TECHNICAL INDEXES

The purpose of any index is to find information. For most subjects, quantifying the value of finding information is subjective. However, for the computer industry, we *can* quantify the benefits of a good index.

Based on information from the Society for Technical Communication (STC), in 2001 the average technical support telephone call cost a company $15 to $25. Since that was a few years ago, we'll assume our average support call now costs $25. Let's guess, conservatively, that in a single year, 10 percent of your customers call with a question or problem instead of finding the answer in the manual. If you've sold 5,000 copies of your software, that's 500 calls in a year. At a cost of $25 for each call, your company has spent $12,500 on technical support in one year.

In contrast, a well-written index for that same manual costs $600 to $1,200 (assuming a length of 200–300 pages and a per page rate between $3 and $4). If the index helps half of the users find the information, the company has saved $6,250. And that's only for one year.

Obviously, the numbers for each product will vary, but these kinds of calculations can be very useful when marketing your services to computer companies. I have done some informal research on this issue with my computer-industry friends and acquaintances. I asked how they approached computer manuals. No one read them from front to back. The usual procedure involved opening the box and putting the manual on a shelf where it collects dust until something goes wrong. When that happens, the first reaction is to consult the index to find the needed information.

The computer business is known for its high-speed, constant innovation. Developers don't have time to spend looking for information. They want it available—NOW!

This makes indexes especially appreciated and our work valuable, once we translate its value into dollars and cents.

COMPUTER TERMINOLOGY

If you've ever tried to read your computer's documentation, you know the computer industry has its own language. Unfortunately, this language is always changing, full of specialized terminology and confusing jargon.

This leads us to some specific problem areas.

Acronyms

DLL, COM, DRAM, API, HTML, URL, MFC, CLSID, ATL, RFID, OOP, GUID, XML, SQL, ASCII, and so on. These are all acronyms used in the computer industry. That list only scratches the surface, and new ones are generated every day. How should you index them?

Nancy Mulvany, in *Indexing Books,*[1] gives good advice, which boils down to this:

- If the acronym is widely known to the book's audience, use the acronym only. Example: ASCII.

- If the acronym is not widely known, help the reader find the information by putting it both under the acronym and under the full name as in either of the following two examples (depending on how many locators there are):

> DLLs (Dynamic Link Libraries), 19, 47, 105
> Dynamic Link Libraries (DLLs), 19, 47, 105

Or
> DLLs (Dynamic Link Libraries)
>   creating, 47, 102 543
>   linking to, 105–117
>   using existing, 121–125, 543–544
> Dynamic Link Libraries (DLLs) see DLLs

The *Chicago Manual of Style*[2] (15th edition) includes a brief explanation of the use of acronyms in 18.46:

> Organizations that are widely known under their abbreviations should be indexed and alphabetized according to the abbreviations. Parenthetical glosses, cross-references, or both should be added if the abbreviations, however familiar to the indexer, may not be known to all readers of the particular work. Lesser-known organizations are better indexed under the full name, with a cross-reference from the abbreviation if it is used frequently in the work.

Expert Tip

Sometimes, it's easy to lose track of an acronym's meaning or the author may neglect to include them. Thankfully, due to the Internet, it's easy to look many of them up. Here are some sites that can help:

www.acronymfinder.com

www.gurunet.com

www.instantweb.com

URLs

URLs (Uniform Resource Locators) are the Internet addresses for Web sites. An Internet address (for example, http://www.hmco.com/trade) usually consists of the access protocol (http), the domain name (www.hmco.com), and optionally the path to a file or resource residing on that server (/trade).

Many books on computer information provide URLs to allow readers to get more information on the author, related technology, sample applications, and so forth. This kind of information can be useful to include in the index.

Selecting the headings for the information should be done just as you would for any other subject. However, you may want to provide access points at the locations:

- Web addresses

- Internet addresses

- Online information

A link to the author's personal Web site (http://www.joesmith.com) might require these entries:

> Internet addresses
> > author's site, 5
>
> .
>
> .
>
> .
>
> online information. See Internet addresses
> Smith, Joe, 5
> Web addresses. See Internet addresses

References to Internet/Web

Since "Internet" and "Web" are proper names, they should always be capitalized. Also the correct terms are "Web site" and "Web page." However, I've seen computer documentation refer to "websites." In this case, I recommend discussing the usage with your editor. However, if this is the term used in the text, you should also use it in the index.

SORTING

Entries Starting with Numbers

Index headings starting with numbers are common in computer information. In most indexes, where entries starting with numbers are infrequent, these entries are sorted as though they are spelled out (e.g., 19 sorted as "nineteen" in the N's). In computer books, since many more entries start with numbers, I've found that most users expect these entries to appear at the beginning of the index. Assuming you have room, help your index user by double-posting these locators in both places. If space is tight, put all entries starting with numbers at the beginning of the index above the letter A.

Entries Starting with Symbols

Sometimes computer subjects include discussions of terms that start with a symbol instead of a letter or number. These include things like file extensions (.jpg or .htm) or programming terms (++ or <=).

File extensions can usually be handled as in this example:

.bmp files, 215
.dll files, 147, 201
.ini files, 14

The word "files" in each heading clarifies the entry and provides needed context. Naturally, the index may also contain these corresponding entries:

bitmap files
DLL files
file types
    bitmap, 215
    DLL, 147, 201
    ini, 14
ini files, 14

For other symbols such as +, &, || or %, which are commonly used as operators in programming languages, these could be listed:

+ (addition operator), 15, 93
& (address of operator), 75
|| (conditional or operator), 95–96
% (modulus operator), 17

These entries are generally sorted before any entries starting with numbers. The gloss (brief explanation of an obscure word or expression) following the symbol provides context and a verbal term for the symbol or the command it represents. For each command, of course, the corresponding verbal term would be added to the index as well. For the example above, the following additional entries would be generated:

addition operator (+), 15, 93

SPECIAL TERMINOLOGY

Documentation of programming languages usually includes key words that make up the syntax of the language. These words come from standard English, but in the context of the programming language, they take on special meaning. This includes words like "AND," "continue," and "integer."

Computer books often incorporate code examples. To distinguish the text that makes up the program code from the normal text, some publishers use different fonts for the code. I often see a serif font used for normal text with a san serif font for code. The same distinction can be used in the index. However, in the index I've found that the font distinction often gets lost. I prefer an explanatory term or a gloss here as well.

INDEXING COMMAND NAMES

When documenting development environments or APIs (Application Programming Interfaces), you usually need to index items such as commands, functions, classes, or controls. There can be lots of these.

When indexing items like functions, my preference is to list each item individually as a main heading. Under the main heading Functions, I list information about the group as a whole.

I've also seen each item repeated as subentries under a main heading Functions. In my opinion, this process usually works only if a few functions are discussed. Otherwise, there's a huge list of subentries that consumes a lot of space. A good alternative to this approach is to include a generic cross-reference such as *See also specific commands.*

COMPLEX SUBJECT RELATIONSHIPS

Complex subject relationships—a common occurence in computer books as well as in scholarly books—are entries with more than two levels of complexity. If your index is limited to a single level of subentry, representing these relationships adequately can be problematic. See the example:

Expert Tip

My preference:
functions
    creating, 76
    member, 86–95
    virtual, 82
    See also specific function names
GetParentFrame function, 76
GetStatus function, 105

However, space permitting, you could do this (especially if the book doesn't discuss lots and lots of specific functions):
functions
    creating, 76
    GetParentFrame function, 76
    GetStatusFunction, 105
    member, 86–95
    virtual, 82
GetParentFrame function, 76
GetStatus function, 105

databases
    backing up, 25, 196
    closing, 17
    creating
        by copying existing, 25, 33, 45
        by designing tables, 26–32, 33, 98–200
        from templates, 23–24, 78, 206
    documenting, 82
    linking to, 176–177, 187

The information, represented here in three levels, seems very straightforward. However, this method is not an option if you are limited to two index levels. Some alternatives are:

Option 1:   databases
            backing up, 25, 196

closing, 17
creating. See databases, creating
documenting, 82
linking to, 176–177, 187
databases, creating
by copying existing, 25, 33, 45
by designing tables, 26-32, 33, 98–200
from templates, 23–24, 78, 206

Comments: This option has everything together, but the index user may not see the second main head "databases, creating" and miss those entries.

Option 2:   databases
backing up, 25, 196
closing, 17
creating by copying existing, 25, 33, 45
creating by designing tables, 26–32, 33, 98–200
creating from templates, 23–24, 78, 206
documenting, 82
linking to, 176–177, 187

Comments: Out of the three options, this is my favorite. This option groups everything together nicely but the subentries starting with "creating" are a bit long for easy readability.

Option 3:   creating databases
by copying existing, 25, 33, 45
by designing tables, 26–32, 33, 98–200
from templates, 23–24, 78, 206
databases
backing up, 25, 196
closing, 17
creating. See creating databases
documenting, 82
linking to, 176–177, 187

Comments: This is my least favorite choice. If the index user is looking for information on creating databases, he would look under databases, see the cross-reference, and then have to perform the additional step of going to a different page in the index to find "creating databases." At least in Option 1, the cross-reference is immediately next to the current main head, which saves the reader from having to search for another main heading.

GERUNDS AND COMPUTER INDEXING

The *Chicago Manual of Style* defines a gerund as a "present participle used as a noun." In turn, it indicates that "the present participle denotes the verb's action as in progress or incomplete" and "the present participle invariably ends in *ing*." My definition of a gerund is a verb that has been altered by the addition of "ing" and which is used as a noun. For example, in the sentence "Creating indexes is fun" the phrase "creating indexes" is a gerund because it functions as a noun. In the sentence "Here are the files that we are deleting," "deleting" is not a gerund because it does not serve as a noun.

In computer books, gerunds come up frequently in concepts like "creating," "closing," and "opening" as in:

> applications
> > opening, 14
> > closing, 28
> > creating, 228–235
>
> cancel print job command, 42
> closing applications, 28
> deleting
> > files, 33
> > print jobs, 42
>
> creating
> > applications, 228–235
> > files, 26–27
>
> files
> > creating, 26–27
> > opening, 18–23
> > deleting, 33
>
> opening
> > applications, 14
> > files, 18–23

Notice how the indexer has swapped the subheadings and main headings. This allows the user to find the information on how to create a file by looking either under *files* or *creating*. The researcher can find the information no matter which term they pick.

There has been and will probably continue to be much disagreement among indexers about the use of gerunds in indexes. Some indexers, concerned about the clarity and readability of entries in the example above, would prefer entries such as:

> applications
> > opening, 14

> closing, 28
> creating, 228–235
> cancel print job command, 42
> closing applications, 28
> deleting files, 33
> deleting print jobs, 42
> creating applications, 228–235
> creating files, 26–27
> files
>> creating, 26–27
>> opening, 18–23
>> deleting, 33
> opening applications, 14
> opening files, 18–23

Either method can work and the one you choose will depend on the text, the editor, and your own preferences.

If you (or the publisher) choose to avoid gerunds entirely, you can alter these entries to read like this:

> applications
>> how to open, 14
>> how to close, 28
>> how to create, 228–235
> cancel print job command, 42
> deletion of files, 33
> deletion of print jobs, 42
> creation of applications, 228–235
> creation of files, 26–27
> files
>> how to create, 26–27
>> how to open, 18–23
>> how to delete, 33

Personally, I find the no-gerund version rather awkward, but you may disagree. As with most other indexing issues, the correct solution depends on a lot of different factors. It's up to the indexer to choose the best solution.

EVALUATING THE INDEX

As a software engineer and user interface designer, I learned a lot about how to tell if my software was meeting the index user's needs. The best technique is called usability testing. And, fortunately, usability testing can be applied to more than just software. It can also serve to evaluate any index. What's more, it doesn't take long and is practically free.

Usability Testing in Six Easy Steps

1. Decide on the structure of your index. Create the index including the major headings and subs. At this point, it doesn't matter if the locators are correct or not, so if you're pressed for time, make up locators so you can get the testing done.

2. Select test subjects. Keeping your readers in mind, select three or four people who have a range of knowledge and experience comparable to the readers. For example, if you're indexing a book on how to use Windows for first-time computer users, select people who've never used a computer. For an advanced programming book on components, choose developers with lots of experience.

3. Set specific, quantifiable goals. If your goal is to make terms easy to find, that's nice but it's not measurable. How would you quantify this? One possible goal would be for your readers to find an entry that will lead them to the information within 30 seconds. With this goal, it's easy to say whether the index passed or failed.

4. Develop a list of three or four test questions. Here are some examples:

   • How would you use the index to find out how much space you have remaining on your hard drive?

   • How does a new GUID get assigned when you create a new component?

5. Meet with each test subject one on one. Explain that you are testing the index, not them. Ask them to complete each task while talking about what they are doing. For example, if I ask an index user to find out how much space is remaining on a hard drive, I want them to say something like "Okay, I'd look up hard drive. Well, there's several items here. Oh, look, there's an entry that says 'finding space remaining.'" Time how long it takes. Testing each subject will take less than five minutes, and you'll be amazed how consistent the results are.

6. Evaluate. If you get a result like that in step 5 within your goal time, you know your index is working. If the users can't find the information, get stuck or frustrated, or take too much time, that tells you that you need to rethink the structure of the index or that your terminology is probably not congruent with the user's level of knowledge.

And that's it. If your results are good, you're ready to finalize your index with confidence that it will really work. If not, rethink your approach, make the changes and test again, preferably with different subjects.

And the cost? I've had very good response to homemade cookies—not too high a price to pay for an index that will be really useful and in which you will have confidence.

Expert Tip

My favorite book, unfortunately now out of print, on the subject is TOG *on Interface by Bruce Tognazzini. Published in 1992 by Addison-Wesley, it's a surprisingly entertaining book describing how to design user interfaces. Along the way, the author goes into detail about his approach to usability testing. He also includes a very interesting discussion about personality types (à la Myers-Briggs) and how they can lead to lapses in communication. It may still be available via online used book sources such as http://www.powells.com or http://www. abebooks.com.*

AND THE FINAL CONSENSUS IS...

As you can see, indexing computer-related subjects is not that different from other kinds of indexing. With a willingness to learn new technology and terminology, and a few specific changes to your indexing techniques, you too can index these kinds of subjects. As with any other subject, if you remember to represent the interests of your index users and do your best to meet their needs, you will be successful.

ENDNOTES

1. Nancy C. Mulvany. *Indexing Books*. Chicago: University of Chicago Press, 1994. pp. 128–130.
2. *Chicago Manual of Style*, 15th ed. Chicago: University of Chicago Press, 2003.

Chapter 8

Web Indexes and Other Navigation Aids: Finding Information on Web Sites

Fred Brown © 2005

OVERVIEW

This chapter explores different applications of indexing to making information findable on Web sites. Indexing is defined broadly as being any type of human mediation in creating the search structure.

Jean-Luc Doumont (STC Web seminar, "Effective Web Sites," January 2004) stated that a navigation scheme provides a map that helps you:

- Know where you are, and

- Make decisions about where to go next.

This chapter focuses on online "maps" for information retrieval within Web sites—not the Internet as whole. This focus is analogous to looking at a single document or document set. I will examine different implementations and explore how they work—in other words, a sort of "show and tell." My goal is to get an overall sense of what types of Web indexing and navigation aids exist and what they can do.

WEB INDEXES

Web indexes look a lot like their back-of-the-book cousins, only the reference locators (page numbers in books) are hypertext-linked. The index heading itself may be hyperlinked or there may be a string of hyperlinked reference locators following the heading.

Web indexes offer the many advantages of back-of-the-book indexes. Indexes can locate information in different ways and they bring together scattered references. Just as back-of-the-book indexes are a familiar tool to book readers, Web site indexes will become familiar to online readers.

Because back-of-the-book indexes are a familiar tool to book readers, the format aids in understanding the online style. When a new technology is developed, it's natural to copy existing forms and later to develop the new potential in different ways, as will be shown for example in Topic Maps. The Linus Pauling Research Notes in Figure 8.1 represent an example of a direct transfer of the back-of-the-book index model to the online world.

Linus Pauling Research Notes

http://osulibrary.orst.edu/specialcollections/rnb

Linus Pauling keeps track of details of scientific research in a wide variety of fields. Notes include laboratory calculations, experimental data, scientific calculations, ideas for further research, and autobiographical musings. Figure 8.1 shows a sample page.

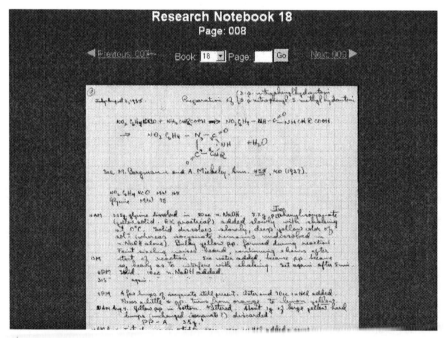

Figure 8.1   Linus Pauling notebook page

   The notebook pages have been converted directly into a graphic format for viewing on the Web. Full-text searching is not feasible. The index thus acts as the central tool for locating material in the notebooks. Figure 8.2 shows the menu for the index, in alphabetical order as we would expect.

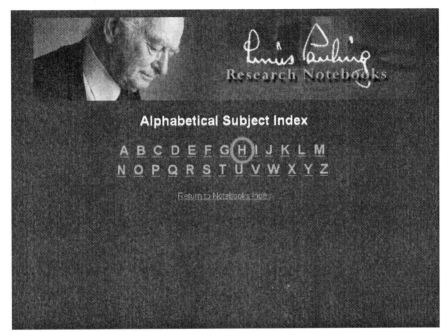

Figure 8.2   Linus Pauling index menu

   Clicking on the letter H brings up the index headings under H as shown in Figure 8.3. Notice that the reference locator consists of both the book number and a page number or range. For example, the index subheading "Methane bond angles" has the reference locator consisting of 23 for the notebook (like a volume number) and the page range (175–176)—very much like a back-of-the-book index!

Parliament of Australia
http://www.aph.gov.au
   The Parliament of Australia distributes information related to the activities of the Parliament of Australia—Hansard, committee reports, bills, and so on—a substantial and changing site. The back-of-the-book index now acts as a "metaphor." A metaphor uses a model from one context (e.g., the printed book) to help you understand how to function in another context (e.g., a Web site). For example, Apple used the "desk top" metaphor to help consumers intuitively understand how to use their

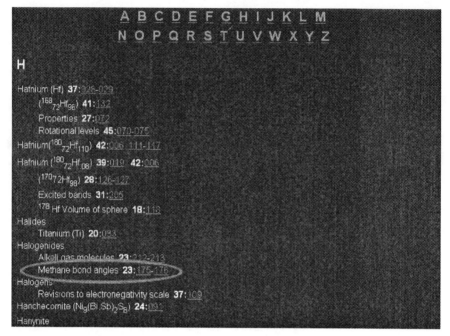

Figure 8.3   Index headings under the letter H

computers. While the Linus Pauling Research Notes directly copy the back-of-the-book model to the online world, the Parliament of Australia index makes some fundamental changes while retaining the familiar look and feel of the back-of-the-book index.

The Parliament of Australia index provides an interface to "gateway pages" which contain the detailed links. Gateway pages provide a set of links to other pages as opposed to the information or content. The Parliament of Australia index doesn't take you directly to the page with the information but rather to a smaller, more focused set of material in a gateway page where you can search. Ongoing updates are made to the gateway pages thus allowing the Web index to remain fairly stable. This approach provides the familiarity and ease of use of the back-of-the-book index while remaining fairly stable and being short enough to browse through online.

Figure 8.4 shows the first page of the Parliament of Australia Index. Clicking on the letter E brings up the headings under E as shown in Figure 8.5.

Each heading that is hyperlinked is linked to only one Web page, thus eliminating the need to show reference locators. Multiple links would necessitate locators following each index entry as are used in the Linus Pauling index. The result is a very clean and understandable design. Clicking on "E-briefs on Hot Issues" goes to the gateway page shown in Figure 8.6.

Clicking on the title "Indigenous Broadcasting" now goes to a subsection of the Web site (Figure 8.7). The Web visitor still has some searching to do. What the Web

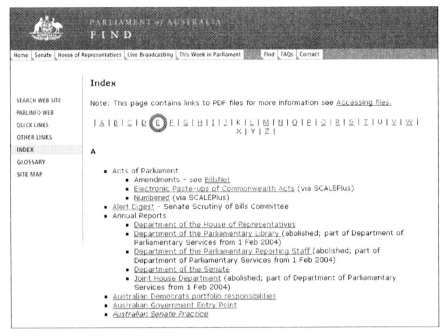

Figure 8.4   Parliament of Australia index first page

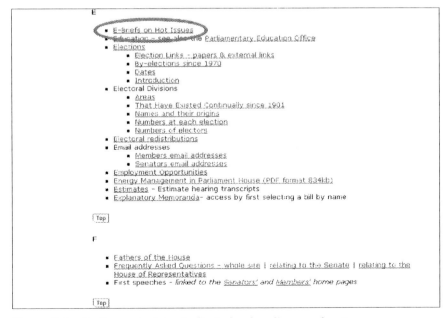

Figure 8.5   Parliament of Australia index headings under E

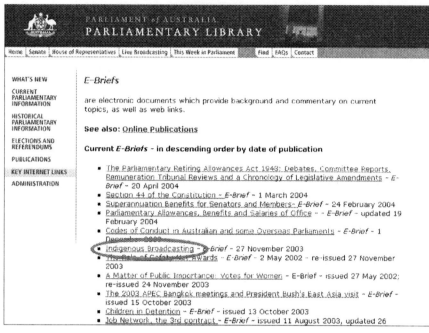

Figure 8.6   Parliament of Australia gateway page

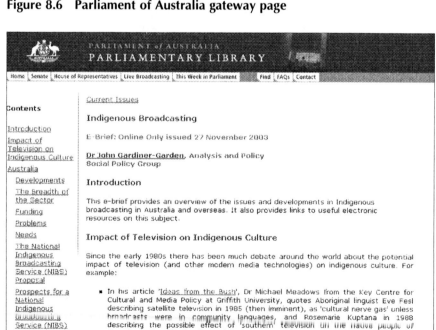

Figure 8.7   Parliament of Australia Web site section

index and accompanying gateway pages have done is to narrow the visitor's search area into a manageable bit.

European Commission
http://europa.eu.int/comm/atoz_en.htm
   This multilingual index with a simple single level structure helps with translation. Index headings link to gateway pages.

AI Topics
http://www.aaai.org/AITopics/html/welcome.html
   This Web site contains more than 100 thematic pages—with both discussion and resource links. The Web index acts as an interface to the thematic pages. It is also interwoven with a top-down subject list.

In summary, Web indexes:

- Provide multiple ways to find a given topic.
- Are easily browseable.
- Compile all references to a given topic under a single heading.
- Combine two or more terms together in advance for the user (pre-coordination).
- Are well-understood by users.
- Work well for small, relatively static bodies of information.
- Create stable, simple interface to gateway pages.

SINGLE HIERARCHIES

Single hierarchies are often called taxonomies, directories, or subject lists. Please note that "taxonomy" can also refer to any system for defining controlled terminology and their relationships. Taxonomies, directories, and subject lists have a single, central hierarchy, much like the roots of a tree. A back-of-the-book index, on the other hand, may contain many small hierarchies and so appears more as a forest of hierarchies.

Taxonomies are used in biology to describe hierarchical groupings of related plants or animals. The following example of the National Center for Biotechnology Information shows an extensive taxonomy for cellular organisms.

National Center for Biotechnology Information
http://www.ncbi.nlm.nih.gov/Taxonomy/Browser/wwwtax.cgi?mode=Root

The National Center for Biotechnology Information provides a database on cellular organisms on its Web site. This hierarchy is very wide and goes down at least eight levels.

Figure 8.8 shows the top level of the taxonomy: Archaea, Bacteria, Eukaryota, Viroids, Viruses, and Other Unclassified.

Clicking on Eukaryota reveals a wide hierarchy as shown in Figure 8.9.

Clicking on "Apusomonas proboscidea" brings us to a summary of this microorganism as shown in Figure 8.10.

The summary confirms Apusomonas proboscidea's lineage in the hierarchy: cellular organisms->Eukaryota->Apusomonadidae->Apusomonas.

U.S. Census Bureau

http://www.census.gov

The U.S. Census Bureau was one of the first government agencies to offer a Web portal. The portal provides researchers and the general public with direct access to a vast array of statistics and analysis. The home page features a subject list with major themes and broad subtopics—a simple, clear, top-down structure—as shown in Figure 8.11. The major topics such as "Business" lead to broad gateway pages, while subtopics such as "Income" link to more specific gateway pages.

Figure 8.12 shows the gateway page linked to the "Business" topic. The gateway page contains many links to detailed information.

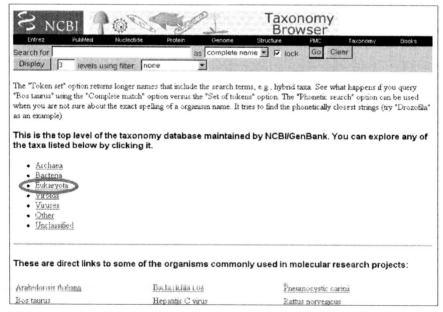

Figure 8.8   National Center for Biotechnology (NCB) top level

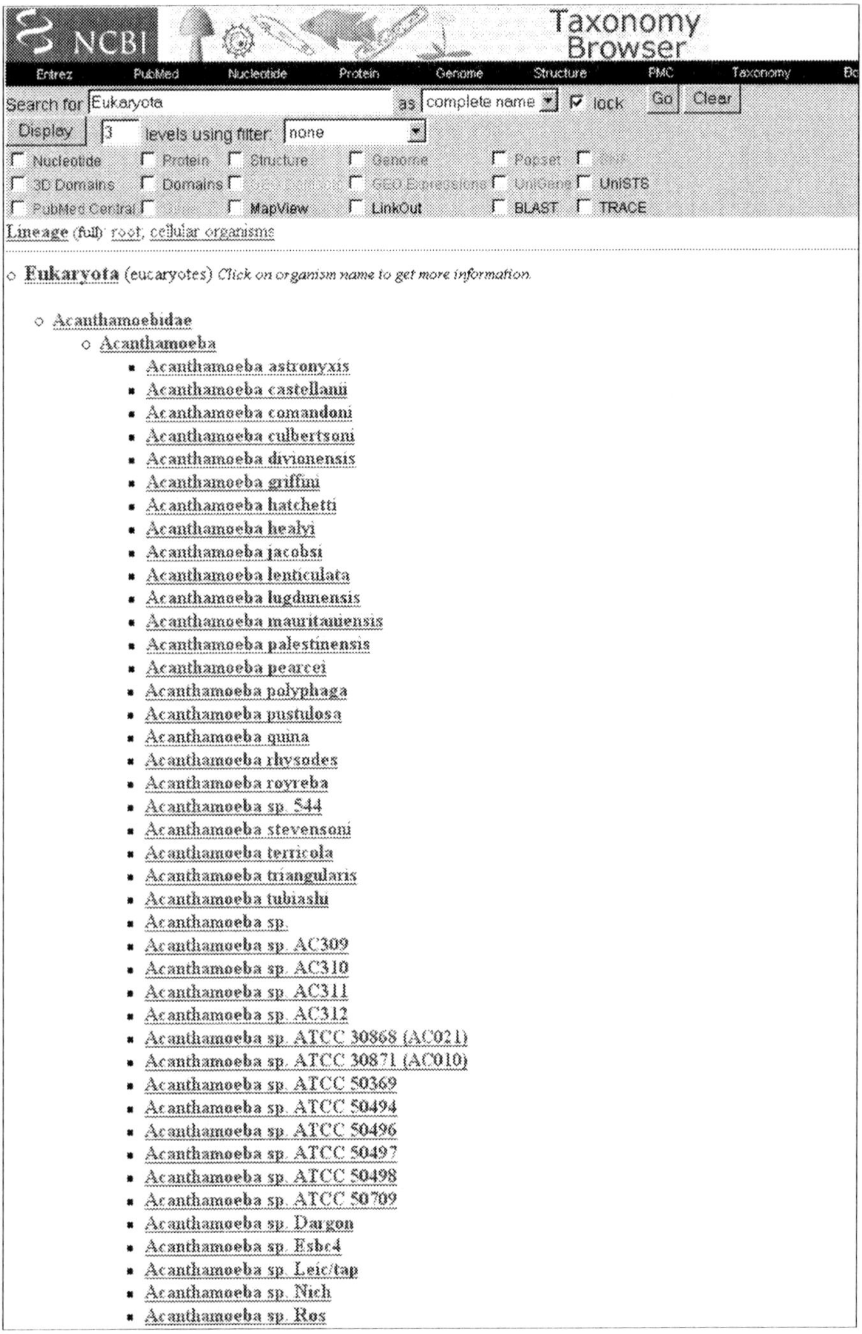

Figure 8.9 Eukaryota

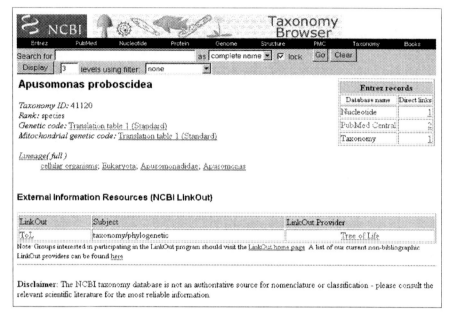

Figure 8.10   **Apusomonas proboscidea**

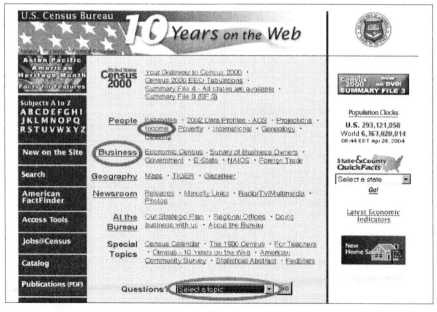

Figure 8.11   **U.S. Census Bureau home page**

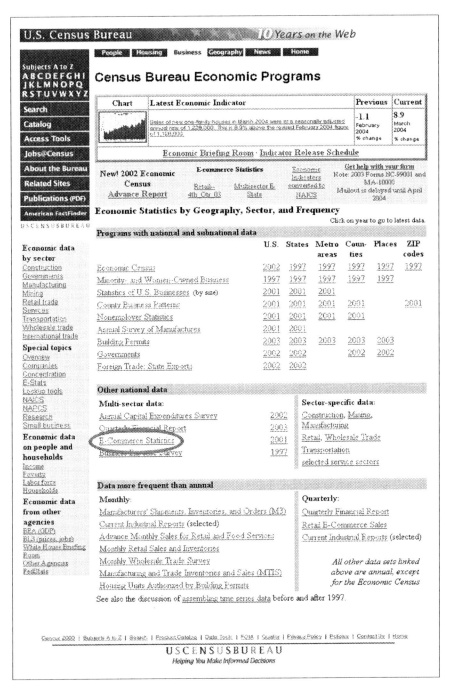

Figure 8.12   U.S. Census Bureau business gateway page

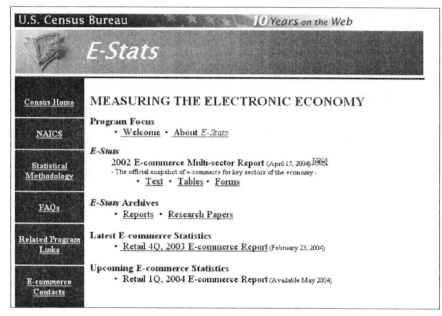

Figure 8.13   U.S. Census Bureau e-commerce statistics

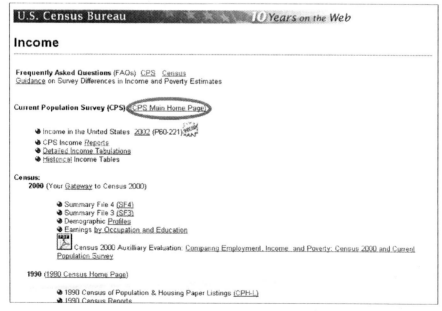

Figure 8.14   U.S. Census Bureau income gateway page

Clicking on "E-Commerce Statistics" will take you to the specific subsection of the Web portal about that subject, as shown in Figure 8.13.

The "income" subtopic shown in Figure 8.11 leads to a minor gateway page, as shown in Figure 8.14.

Much like the Parliament of Australia site, the U.S. Census Bureau portal uses gateway pages to store internal links that are updated while the subject list or Web index remains static.

Culture.ca

http://www.culture.ca/canada

Culture.ca attempts to make Canadian culture—both English-speaking and French-speaking—accessible on the Web. It acts as a gateway to Canadian cultural Web sites and contains a database of more than 6,000 cataloged Web sites (Figure 8.15).

The hierarchical taxonomy is implemented through a series of layered menus in the upper left-hand corner. Clicking on "Media and Publishing" brings up a submenu as shown in Figure 8.16. The list may be a little long for just browsing through as it contains 133 films.

Clicking on "Film" brings up a final sub-sub menu, as shown in Figure 8.17.

Clicking on "Astor Theatre" brings you to an actual resource as shown in Figure 8.18.

The site employs a straightforward "intuitive" taxonomy to help visitors find Web resources in the database. However, the Web resources are catalogued using the Dewey Decimal system. The Dewey Decimal categories are then mapped to the Web site taxonomy terms. This mapping allows the taxonomy to evolve without having to change how the Web site resources are cataloged.

In summary, single hierarchies:

- Look like tables of contents.
- Typically provide only one way or path for finding a given topic.
- Are browseable.
- Make it easy to find information if you understand the structure, but can be frustrating if you don't.
- Gather together all references to a given topic under a single heading.
- Work well for large bodies of information.

METADATA

I use a narrow definition of "metadata"—data about a collection of resources such as Web sites, services, or people. Metadata looks like an "electronic" library

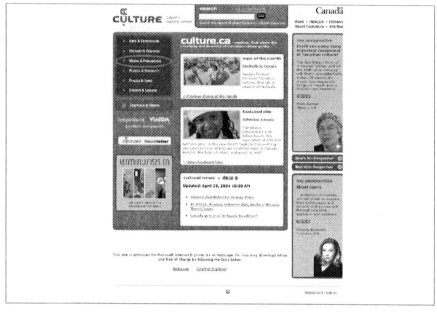

Figure 8.15   Culture.ca home page

Figure 8.16   Culture.ca film sub-menu

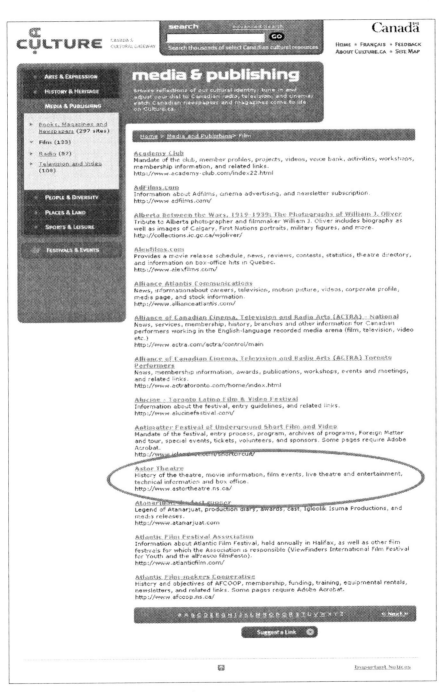

Figure 8.17   Culture.ca list of films

Figure 8.18   Astor Theatre

of catalogue cards, defining fields such as title, author, document type, subject, and copyright. Metadata fields can be categorized in three groups:

- Descriptive (content): author, subject
- Administrative metadata (management): copyright, lifecycle
- Structural: file format

ADAM (Art, Design, Architecture & Media Information Gateway)
http://adam.ac.uk/index.html

ADAM is an Internet catalog or "virtual library" to cultural resources for higher education in the U.K. It integrates a subject list and a thesaurus into the metadata structure.

Figure 8.19 shows results for search, involving three fields: Historical Period, Resource Type, and ADAM Subject Headings ("Design" selected). ADAM offers a choice of its own subject headings or terms from the *Art & Architecture Thesaurus* (The J. Paul Getty Trust).

Clicking on the first search result brings up the full bibliographic record, as shown in Figure 8.20.

ADAM Search Results: 11 Records

Click here for records 11 onwards...

CLEAR SEARCH   **Scroll down to view search results**

About ADAM

Historical Period:
2000-2999 AD

Search & Browse

Resource Type:
Public & Non-profit Bodies

Friends of ADAM

ADAM Subject Headings	Art & Architecture Thesaurus
Top	Associated Concepts
Design	Attributes and Properties
Fashion Design	Built Complexes and
General Design	Districts
Graphic Design	Color
Industrial	Components
Interior Design	Conditions and Effects
Product and Packaging	Containers
Design	Costume
	Design Elements
	Disciplines
	Events
	Exchange Media
	Functions
	Furnishings
	Information Forms
	Materials
	Measuring Devices
	Object Genres
	Object Groupings and
	Systems
	Open Spaces and Site
	Elements
	Organizations
	People
	Physical Activities
	Processes and Techniques
	Recreational Artifacts
	Settlements and
	Landscapes
	Single Built Works
	Sound Devices
	Styles and Periods
	Tools and Equipment
	Transportation Vehicles
	Visual Works
	Weapons and Ammunition

Nominate a site

Site map & search

1.   Adaptive Environments Center Home Page

Web site of the Adaptive Environments Center, founded to address the environmental issues that confront disabled and elderly people. The Center promotes accessibility and universal design through education, technical assistance and design advocacy. The site provides details of these, and links to many universal design and disability resources.

Subjects 745.2; 711.087; Adaptive Environments Center; universal design; product design; aged; Design; industrial design; housing for the handicapped; housing for the elderly; education; Public & Non-profit Bodies

ROADS   890660505-11442
URI   http://www.adaptenv.org/
Details   View full ADAM record

2.   William Morris Society

Web site devoted to William Morris and sponsored by the William Morris Society. Gathers together news of Morris-related events and publications; information about the worldwide William Morris Society; materials relating to the life and work of Morris, his friends and followers in the Arts and Crafts Movement; and links to other sites of interest.

Subjects 745.4492 MOR; 709.034; 19th Century 1800-1899; Morris, William; William Morris Society; wallpaper; book illustration;

Figure 8.19   ADAM search results

Searching ADAM Database

Step through your
result set

Adaptive Environments Center Home Page

Web site of the Adaptive Environments Center, founded to address the
environmental issues that confront disabled and elderly people. The
Center promotes accessibility and universal design through education,
technical assistance and design advocacy. The site provides details of
these, and links to many universal design and disability resources.

ROADS	890660505-11442
URI	http://www.adaptenv.org/
ASH	Design
Organisations	Adaptive Environments Center
General	universal design; product design; aged; industrial design; housing for the handicapped; housing for the elderly; education
Resource Type	Public & Non-profit Bodies
DDC21	745.2; 711.087

About ADAM

Search & Browse

Friends of ADAM

Nominate a site

Figure 8.20   ADAM full bibliographic record

The metadata in the bibliographic record includes a description, location on the
Web, creator (organization), and Dewey Decimal Number in addition to the search
fields.

Africa Focus: Sights and Sounds of a Continent
http://africafocus.library.wisc.edu

Africa Focus contains a database of images and sounds from Africa. It was developed by the Africa Studies Program of the University of Wisconsin-Madison. You
can browse or search using single or multiple categories.

Figure 8.21 shows the browse interface in which the photos and sound clips are
grouped by theme. Clicking on "Artisans" brings you to the set of photos for that
theme as shown in Figure 8.22.

Figure 8.23 shows the 0121jt01 photo record including some of the metadata
fields.

Figure 8.24 shows the search interface. Note that it also includes structural metadata such as the file type (for example, Real Audio or JPEG).

In summary, metadata:

- Provides structured information about a collection of resources.

- Is structured in a "schema" containing defined fields.

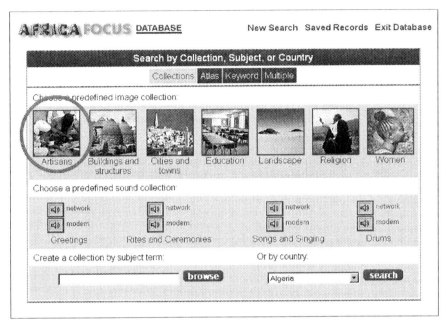

Figure 8.21   Africa Focus browse interface

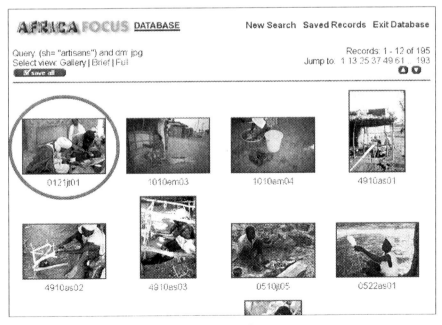

Figure 8.22   Africa Focus Artisan theme photos

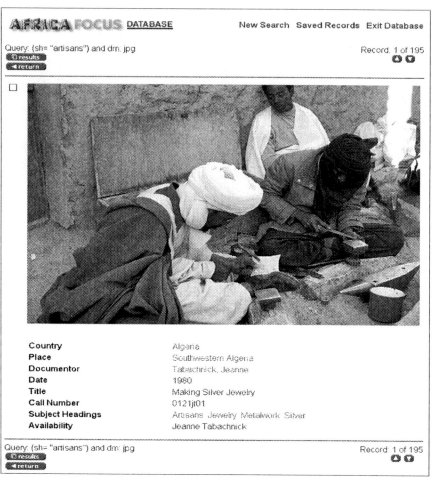

Figure 8.23   Africa Focus photo record

- May be linked to thesauri, taxonomies, or other standards.
- Is used largely for searching but can be used for browsing as well.

TOPIC MAPS

Topic maps are the newest "baby on the block." They are based on topics and relationships between topics. As in back-of-the-book indexing, topics can be actual physical things or abstract concepts. A wide variety of relationships can be defined and

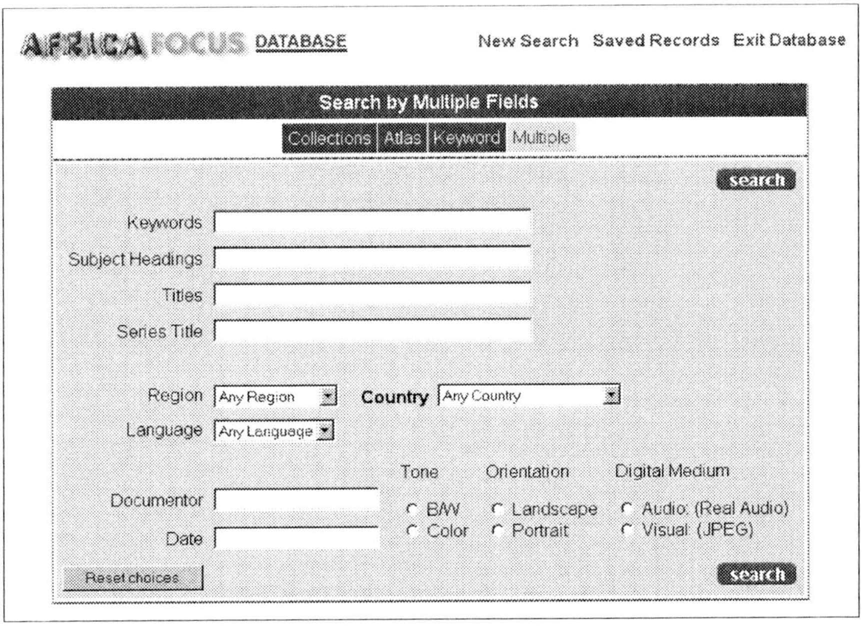

Figure 8.24   Africa Focus search screen

used. Topic maps offer flexibility in terms of being able to model a search structure. They reflect object-oriented analysis applied to indexing.

The following example illustrates how topic maps can assist index users to navigate a set of information. You can also observe how the information is organized in terms of topics and relationships.

Scripts and Languages

http://www.ontopia.net/i18n/index.jsp

"Scripts" refers to alphabets such as Cyrillic, Arabic, or Roman. The site looks at relationships between scripts and the languages that use them. Figure 8.25 shows the structure of the topic map.

The visual diagram on the right is similar to entity-relationship models in the object-oriented world. "Scripts" (a topic or class) is "used to write" (an association or relationship) a "language" (a topic or class). The list of fields on the left provides different ways of viewing or organizing the data.

Clicking on "by language" pulls up a list, as shown in Figure 8.26.

"Dzongkha" is a specific language—or instance of the topic "Language." Clicking on "Dzongkha" reveals specific information about this language, as shown in Figure 8.27.

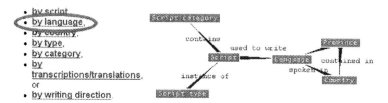

Scripts and languages

This is a site about the scripts of the world, and the languages they are used to write. The site provides information about the scripts and languages with links to other sites with in-depth descriptions of each. The site is a web application developed using **the Ontopia Navigator framework**, based on a topic map written by hand by **Lars Marius Garshol**.

The site contains information about 175 different scripts, which you can access through several different indexes. On the right you can see the site structure visualized.

- by script,
- **by language,**
- by country,
- by type,
- by category,
- by transcriptions/translations, or
- by writing direction.

You can also do a **structured search** for the scripts you are interested in, or do a simple full-text search:

Search

Figure 8.25   Scripts and languages home page

Figure 8.26   List of languages

Figure 8.27   Dzongkha script

We can see that Dzongkha "is spoken in" (an association) "Bhutan" (an instance of the topic "Country"). Similarly, Dzongkha "is written in" the "Tibetan script." Clicking on "Tibetan script" reveals information about the Tibetan script, as Figure 8.28 shows.

Clicking on "show family tree" reveals a small hierarchy within the topic map, as shown in Figure 8.29.

In summary, topic maps:

- Model the structure of information in a way similar to object-oriented analysis.

- Consist of topics, associations between topics, and specific instances of the topics themselves.

- Facilitate navigation and searching of a body of information.

- Are highly flexible in terms of types of information structures that can be modeled.

- Work well with large structured bodies of information.

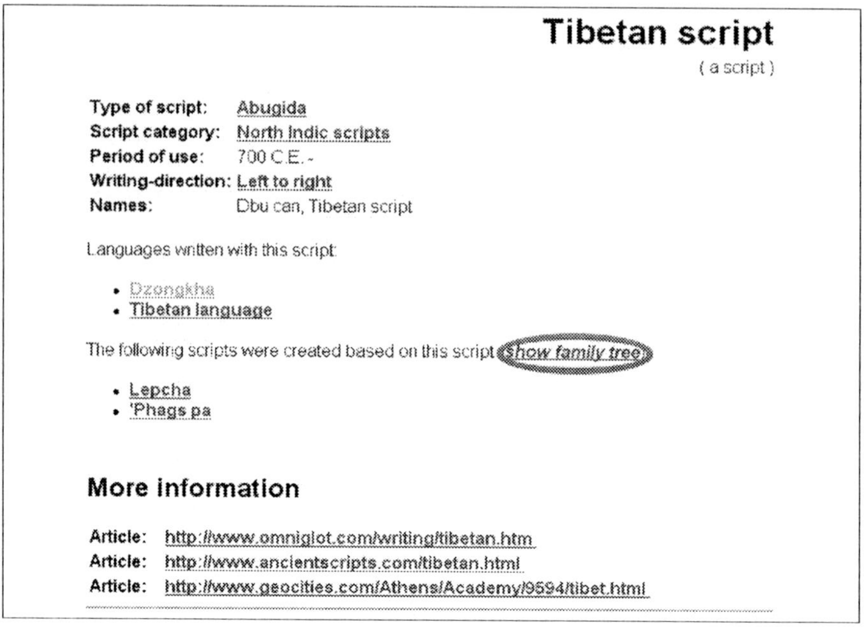

Tibetan script
(a script)
Type of script: Abugida
Script category: North Indic scripts
Period of use: 700 C.E. -
Writing-direction: Left to right
Names: Dbu can, Tibetan script
Languages written with this script:
Dzongkha
Tibetan language
The following scripts were created based on this script (show family tree)
Lepcha
'Phags pa
More information
Article: http://www.omniglot.com/writing/tibetan.htm
Article: http://www.ancientscripts.com/tibetan.html
Article: http://www.geocities.com/Athens/Academy/9594/tibet.html

Figure 8.28 Tibetan script

TOPIC MAPS
top | scripts | languages | countries | types | categories | search
Tibetan script, family tree
Tibetan script
'Phags pa
Lepcha
Lars Marius Garshol, Ontopian

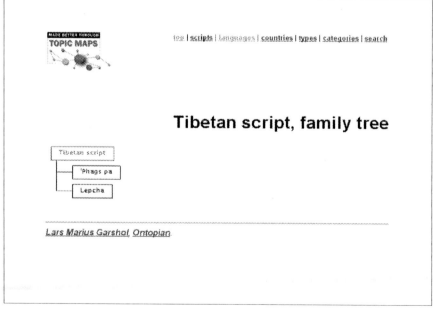

Figure 8.29 Tibetan script, family tree

CONCLUSION

As Jean-Luc Doumont stated, a navigation scheme helps you to know where you are and to be able to make decisions about where to go next. Similarly, this chapter aimed to help you voyage into the evolving realm of Web indexing and navigation aids. The techniques presented employ well-worn models as a foundation on which to build new possibilities. Back-of-the-book style indexes provide a familiar interface for browsing. Taxonomies employ the well-known root structure when digging for data. Metadata harkens back to library card catalogs to provide powerful search capability. Topic maps let you paint your own tableau using a simple palette. I have examined the most common techniques existing today. Hopefully, this chapter will inspire you to paddle your own canoe into new uncharted waters, as more information schemes develop in the future.

RESOURCES

Books

Park, Jack, et al. *XML Topic Maps: Creating and Using Topic Maps for the Web.* Burmingham, UK: Addison-Wesley Professional, 2003.

Professional XML Metadata. Hoboken, NJ: Wrox Press, 2001.

Rosenfield, Louis and Morville, Peter. *Information Architecture for the World Wide Web.* Sebastopol, CA: O'Reilly, 2002.

Web

After the Dot-Bomb: Getting Web Information Retrieval Right This Time
http://firstmonday.dk/issues/issue7_7/bates/index.html

The art of indexing and some fallacies of its automation
http://www.osi.hu/cpd/logos/Theartofindexing.html

Common Look & Feel Metadata Implementation Guides
http://www.nlc-bnc.ca/6/37/s37-4016.001-e.html

Complexity In Indexing Systems—Abandonment And Failure: Implications For Organizing The Internet
http://www.asis.org/annual-96/ElectronicProceedings/weinberg.html

Consideration in Indexing Online Documents
http://www.bwa.org/articles/considerations_in_indexing_online_documents.htm

An Evaluation of Topic Maps (PDF)
http://www.cling.gu.se/~cl8matsn/uppsats.pdf

Dublin Core Metadata Initiative
http://www.dublincore.org

Easy Topic Maps
http://easytopicmaps.com

Faucet Facets: A few best practices for designing multifaceted navigation systems
http://www.adaptivepath.com/publications/essays/archives/000034.php
Global Information Locator Service (GILS)
http://www.gils.net
How To Use HTML Meta Tags
http://searchenginewatch.com/webmasters/meta.html
Indexing Resources on the WWW
http://www.slais.ubc.ca/resources/indexing/database1.htm
Intranet Taxonomy Resource Centre - Web
http://plc.fis.utoronto.ca/coursedescription.asp?courseid=33#
Introduction to Metadata (Web course)
http://www.slis.wisc.edu/academic/ces/webctmeta.html
Metadata: Cataloging by Any Other Name ...
http://www.onlinemag.net/OL1999/milstead1.html
MetaMap
http://mapageweb.umontreal.ca/turner/meta/english
Mind Maps
http://www.infotoday.com/searcher/jun99/humphreys.htm
The TAO of Topic Maps: Finding the Way in the Age of Infoglut
http://www.ontopia.net/topicmaps/materials/tao.html
Thesaurus principles and practice
http://www.willpower.demon.co.uk/thesprin.htm
topicmap.com
http://www.topicmap.com

Contributors

Fred Brown helps to design Web sites and intranets in a way that helps people find information, applying indexing principles to information architecture. His chapter (Chapter 8) is based on presentations given to the Society for Technical Communication (STC) and the Indexing and Abstracting Society of Canada (IASC). Fred has written indexes for book publishers, computer firms, and government agencies. Before succumbing to the love of indexing, he spent a decade writing computer documentation.

Lina B. Burton has a degree in business administration and has pursued postgraduate work in public administration. She is a long-time gardener, Master Gardener, member of ASI's Gardening/Environmental Studies SIG and Culinary SIG, and the Garden Writers Association. Lina discovered she enjoyed indexing when she created the indexes for the two textbooks she wrote, *Office Practices and Procedures* and *Word/Information Processing: Concepts and Applications.* She has been indexing professionally since 1993. Although she is a generalist, she particularly enjoys indexing books on horticulture and cooking. Lina and her husband live in a village in rural Virginia.

Susan DeRenne Coerr of San Francisco has been a freelance indexer and member of ASI since 1984. She particularly enjoys indexing art catalogs, and books on architecture, design, media and popular culture, museology, graphics, history, education, international relations, Latin America, and women's studies. Previous to indexing, during 10 years as a museum registrar, she served as the fifth national president of the Women's Caucus for Art from 1980–1982. Susan holds an MA in Fine Art—Printmaking, and a California State Lifetime Teaching Certificate. She has taught indexing seminars, graduate-level museum documentation, and art and printmaking in college art courses, adult education, and children's art classes.

Marion Lerner-Levine studied liberal arts at the University of Chicago, and drawing and painting at the School of the Art Institute of Chicago. She has been indexing for the last 17 years. For a number of years she worked in-house for Colliers Encyclopedia as an independent contractor, for the annual updating of their volumes. Other publishers for which she has created indexes include Smithsonian Institution Press, Columbia University Press, and St. Martin's Press. Marion has indexed biographies, Santeria esthetics, music, and visual arts to flying saucers, to name a few. She is a professional exhibiting artist as well as an indexer, and lives in Park Slope, Brooklyn, New York.

Kate Mertes is sole proprietor of Mertes Editorial Services, providing indexing, information retrieval, and editorial expertise for complex, challenging projects in law and the humanities. Kate earned her BA in medieval studies, a PhD in medieval history, and a post-doctoral degree in theology, and after teaching at university level for several years moved into publishing. She served on the Board of the American Society of Indexers from 1998 to 2004, and was president of ASI in 2002–2003. She is the current vice-chair of the Washington, DC chapter of ASI. She is also a founding fellow of the Consortium of Indexing Professionals. Some of her recent projects include indexing the Oxford Jewish Study Bible; final editing of the English translation of the Spanish commentary on the Code of Canon Law; developmental editing for a history of the afterlife in the social world of the Abrahamic faiths; and indexing a study of the biography of the Buddhist nun Orgyan Chokyi.

Carrie Nearing is a freelance indexer, editor, and proofreader, with expertise in the areas of law, healthcare, and the social sciences. She received a BA in psychology and political science followed by a degree in law with a special concentration in research and writing. Carrie practiced law in the areas of medical malpractice and healthcare before moving into publishing. She is a member of the American Society of Indexers, the Professional Editors Network in Minneapolis, and the Twin Cities Chapter of ASI.

Beth Palmer's experience in the computer industry spans more than 15 years. She has worked in multiple roles including indexer, software engineer, user interface designer, Web site manager, technical writer/editor, and proofreader. Her educational background includes degrees in both computer science and English Literature. She is active in the Pacific Northwest Chapter of ASI and currently serves as co-Webmaster for the chapter Web site.

Carol Roberts has been indexing since 1993, primarily scholarly books in the humanities, including philosophy. She currently holds the position of secretary on ASI's Board of Directors. She has two master's degrees in philosophy, one from State University of New York at Albany and one from Cornell University.

Thérèse Shere has been a freelance book indexer for eight years. She indexes books of all kinds, but especially plant-related titles and cookbooks. She is particularly interested in the special indexing problems presented by horticultural books and cookbooks, and has developed and taught indexing workshops on both topics. Before becoming an indexer, her professional life revolved around growing and cooking food. She was an organic farmer, co-wrote a kitchen gardening column for *Cook's* magazine with Alice Waters, and co-owned a bakery for 15 years. She lives in Sonoma County, California.

Martin L. White has been an indexer since 1982. His formal education is in mathematics and philosophy, both of which he considers excellent preparation for indexing. He began his indexing career with Encyclopædia Britannica, working as an indexer, indexing supervisor, and in thesaurus development. The index for *Children's Britannica,* for which he was index supervisor, was a runner-up for the Wheatley Medal of the Society of Indexers (U.K.). He has been a freelance indexer since 1990, full time since 1995. Martin specializes in scholarly books, but also indexes trade books, textbooks, and medical journals. His index for John Patrick Diggins' *The Promise of Pragmatism: Modernism and the Crisis of Knowledge and Authority* (University of Chicago Press, 1994) received the 1995 H.W. Wilson Award of the American Society of Indexers for Excellence in Indexing.

Enid L. Zafran has worked as an indexer for more than 25 years. She started in the field of legal publishing working for Banks-Baldwin Law Publishing Co., Prentice-Hall Law & Business, and the Bureau of National Affairs. She began her own indexing business, Indexing Partners, in 1990, and in addition to legal indexing, specializes in public policy, business, art, history, psychology, and education indexing. Enid has served on the Board of the American Society of Indexers and as ASI President (2004–2005). Other ASI publications she edited include *Starting an Indexing Business, Indexing Specialties: Law,* and *Indexing Specialties: Scholarly Books.* Like Kate Mertes, Enid is a founding fellow of the Consortium of Indexing Professionals.

Index

Carrie Nearing

A

Abbreviations, 52
Academic theology, 14, 18, 22
Accents, 20
Acronyms, 110–111
Alphabetization
    biographies, 44–46
    encyclopedias, 51, 58–59
    numbers starting entries, 112–113
    symbols starting entries, 113
Alston, William P., 26
Analytic theology, 18, 19
Anderson, Bernhard W., 24
Apologetics, 20–21
Appiah, Kwame Anthony, 3
Aquinas, Thomas, 13, 22, 25
Archaeology materials, 24–25
Aristotle, 8, 10, 22
Art books/catalogs, 65–83
    art objects, categories of, 67–73
    artists, unknown, 77
    author's knowledge, 74
    captions, 75, 79
    computerized information, 72–73
    confidential information, 70
    date of object creation, 68
    descriptions, 70–71
    fabrication summaries, 70–71
    headings, 79
    history of objects, 70

homographs, 69–70
identification numbers, 71–72
identification of objects, 68–69,
    71–72, 73
illustrations, unnumbered, 78–79
image content, 80
indexable pages, 75
level of detail of indexing, 73–74
medium and material, 69–70
"missing" information, how to han-
    dle, 77–79
museum numbering, 71–72
names, 67–68
number of entries, 75
origin of object, 67–68
plate numbers as references, 79
provenance, 67, 70
recognition description, 71
related artworks, 76–77
resources, 82–83
software programs, 72–73
synonyms, 79
terms of entries, 80
titles
    format of, 68
    organization of, 76–77
types of art books, 65–66
types of media, 70
untitled works, 77–78
writings of artist, 69

More Great Books for Indexing Professionals

Indexing Specialties: Scholarly Books

Edited by Margie Towery and Enid L. Zafran

This skillfully edited book covers the indexing of scholarly books in a number of key fields, including economics, public policy, philosophy, law, and music. The topic of foreign languages in scholarly indexing is given close attention, and John Bealle's account of his experiences in indexing his own work will be welcomed by academic author-indexers. Tying the book together is Margery Towery's essay on what constitutes quality in scholarly indexing.

Softbound • ISBN 1-57387-236-9

ASI Members $28.00 • Nonmembers $35.00

Genealogy and Indexing

Edited by Kathleen Spaltro

Indexes are the essential search tool for genealogists, and this timely book fills a conspicuous void in the literature. Kathleen Spaltro and contributors take an in-depth look at the relationship between indexing and genealogy and explain how genealogical indexes are constructed. They offer practical advice to indexers who work with genealogical documents as well as genealogists who want to create their own indexes. Noeline Bridge's chapter on names will quickly become the definitive reference for trying to resolve questions on variants, surname changes, and foreign designations. Other chapters discuss software, form and entry, the need for standards, and the development of after-market indexes.

Softbound • ISBN 1-57387-163-X

ASI Members $25.00 • Nonmembers $31.25

Software for Indexing

Edited by Sandi Schroeder

In this thorough review of the software products used in indexing, professional indexers share their favorite features, tips, and techniques. Starting with a chapter on dedicated indexing programs, CINDEX, MACREX, SKY Index, and wINDEX are compared. Coverage of embedding software includes Framemaker, Microsoft Word, PageMaker, QuarkXPress, Ixgen, Index Tool Professional, and IndeXTension. For those interested in online and Web indexing, HTML/Prep, HTML Indexer, and RoboHelp are all covered. Other chapters discuss database software, customized software that works with dedicated programs, and automatic and machine-aided indexing.

Softbound • ISBN 1-57387-166-4

ASI Members $28.00 • Nonmembers $35.00

Indexing Specialties: Law

Edited by Peter Kendrick and Enid L. Zafran

This release in the popular "Indexing Specialties" series is devoted to the topic of legal indexing, with contributions from more than a dozen leading practitioners. Part 1, "Getting Started," provides practical advice for new legal indexers and those considering a career in this challenging field. Part 2 covers the ins and outs of "Indexing and Tabling Legal Cases." Maryann Corbett addresses "The Unique Challenges of Indexing Statutory Materials" in Part 3. Part 4 offers a critical assessment of "New Technologies and Methodologies," and the book concludes with Part 5, "Reflections on Legal Indexing," which includes "must-read" chapters by Dorothy Thomas and Kate Mertes. Editors Kendrick and Zafran have created a unique and valuable reference that belongs on the desk of every legal indexer.

Softbound • ISBN 1-57387-113-3

ASI Members $28.00 • Nonmembers $35.00

Indexing Specialties: History

Edited by Margie Towery

This compilation of articles focuses on the indexing of history textbooks, art history, medieval and Renaissance history, Latin American history, and gender and sexual orientation language issues. The authors' intelligent advice and discussions will assist both new and experienced indexers who work in the field of history and related disciplines.

Softbound • ISBN 1-57387-055-2

ASI Members $12.00 • Nonmembers $18.00

Indexing Specialties: Psychology

Edited by Becky Hornyak

Continuing the series that addresses specialized areas for indexers, Becky Hornyak has assembled a panel of experts that includes Sandy Topping, Carolyn Weaver, and Carol Schoun. The emphasis is on indexing textbooks and books aimed at clinical practitioners in the field of psychology. Includes extensive, annotated listings of print and other resources for psychology indexers.

Softbound • ISBN 1-57387-149-4

ASI Members $20.00 • Nonmembers $25.00

To order directly from the publisher, include $4.95 postage and handling for the first book ordered and $1.00 for each additional book. Catalogs also available upon request. Order online at www.infotoday.com and specify that you are an ASI member when ordering.

Information Today, Inc.

143 Old Marlton Pike, Medford, NJ 08055

(800)300-9868   (609)654-6266   custserv@infotoday.com